Praise for John-Francis Friendship

'Fr John-Francis Friendship has gathered together the wisdom of scripture and the saints, from the first centuries of Christianity to the present day, in order to show us the Sacred Heart of Christ which beats with love for every person, and is mystically present throughout creation. This eternal, tender, merciful divine love is expressed with great clarity and articulated with great gentleness. Anglicans, and Christians of all denominations, will find theological and liturgical insights to cherish within this fresh and vibrant book.'

Revd Dr Ayla Lepine SMMS, Associate Rector of St James, Piccadilly, London and author

'In a world where so many seek a home for their hearts, in a world where so many hearts are broken and filled with silent longing, *Heart of My Own Heart* is a beautifully attentive reminder that God's name is Love, and that Jesus is God's love made manifest to us, and to our hearts. This book recapitulates the Christian life as one of honest pilgrimage, of seeking the Love that in Jesus sought and found us. It helps us remember that Christian faith is a spirituality of the heart and Fr John-Francis has powerfully invited readers to allow the heart of Jesus to touch theirs.

There is no greater invitation the church can give than to fall in love with God, and in so doing find ourselves already loved, known and cherished. This is, I believe, the heart of the gospel – it is love, as expounded in this book, that makes

Christian faith credible. *Heart of My Own Heart* makes clear that throughout the Christian tradition, in every age, real human hearts have been taken captive by the Sacred Heart of Jesus, and there found the fullness of the triune love of God.

In this beautiful and timely book, John-Francis shows so clearly that it is the intimacy found in the love of God for us and to us that is the rich ground from which authentic prayer, true penitence and heartfelt praise flow ... and this is an intimacy we need not fear. Oh, how we need to recapture our confidence in the reckless love of God for all today! *Heart of My Own Heart* is good news for the Church and the world.'

Revd Canon Jarel Adrian Robinson-Brown Obl.OSB,
Vicar, St German's, Cardiff, theologian and author

'Writings and testimonies concerning the heart from many traditions have enriched, informed and inspired the writing of this book, giving readers glimpses of that glory revealed through the Sacred Heart of Jesus. John-Francis encourages us, through a synthesis of scripture, poetry and spiritual writings, to a life-transfiguring encounter with this Heart which I really enjoyed reading.'

Sr Rita-Elizabeth SSB, former Superior of the
Society of the Sisters of Bethany

Heart
of My Own
Heart

Heart of My Own Heart

Deepening life with Christ

John-Francis Friendship

CANTERBURY
PRESS

Norwich

© John-Francis Friendship 2024

First published in 2024 by the Canterbury Press Norwich
Editorial office
3rd Floor, Invicta House
110 Golden Lane
London EC1Y 0TG, UK
www.canterburypress.co.uk

Canterbury Press is an imprint of Hymns Ancient & Modern Ltd
(a registered charity)

Hymns Ancient & Modern®

Hymns Ancient & Modern® is a registered trademark of
Hymns Ancient & Modern Ltd
13A Hellesdon Park Road, Norwich,
Norfolk NR6 5DR, UK

Scripture quotations are from the New Revised Standard Version
of the Bible, Anglicized Edition, Copyright © 1989, 1995 by
the Division of Christian Education of the National Council
of the Churches of Christ in the USA. Used by permission.
All rights reserved.
The psalm quotation on page 93 is from *The Psalms: A New
Translation*, Copyright © 1963, The Grail (England), published
by HarperCollins.

British Library Cataloguing in Publication data

A catalogue record for this book is available
from the British Library

978 1 78622 579 5

Typeset by Regent Typesetting
Printed and bound in Great Britain by
CPI Group (UK) Ltd

Expanded Contents

For the purposes of navigation, the following expanded contents list includes text headings

This book is dedicated to the
Sacred Heart of Jesus in the 350th anniversary year
of its apparition to St Margaret-Mary Alacoque
in Paray-le-Monial
and to my partner Chris Marlowe,
who helped open to me the mysteries of entrusting
one's heart to another

Make and awake
a new heart
a true heart
a pure heart
through and through
Christ me
you every crumb of me
love incarnated
God
(Mother Osyth Lucie-Smith OSB, 1898–1992,
sometime Abbess of Malling)

Foreword

by the Rt Revd Gregory Llanelwy

Statues of Jesus with the Sacred Heart emblazoned on his chest are not unfamiliar to those acquainted with Catholic statuary, and can provoke a variety of reactions. To those unfamiliar with the tradition, they can seem rather bizarre and off-putting, while to those who have discovered something of a devotion to the Sacred Heart, and an understanding of the associated spirituality, they can be deeply symbolic of one of the central truths to be proclaimed about God's revelation in Jesus.

John-Francis is a priest who has imbibed deeply at the well of Christian spirituality, developing an expertise in the spiritual life and in spiritual direction through association with the Anglican Franciscans and as a parish priest.

In this book, he engages with the breadth of devotion to the Sacred Heart of Jesus, and invites us to consider what is at the 'heart' of our own Christian faith. At a time when writing about Christian ministry tends to focus on the skills and attitudes that priests need to develop in their exercise of ministry, and the checklist of moral, spiritual and even business accomplishments that are required to resource the successful priest, John-Francis asks us instead to turn to a reflection on our inner life, the spiritual encounter by which 'heart speaks to heart', and how the different dimensions of faith in the heart of God revealed in Jesus can renew and resource our faith and ministry.

John-Francis has a richly stocked mind, and draws on an immense amount of knowledge and experience of spirituality to distil this wisdom for the reader. Ranging across Christian history and spirituality, he draws out lessons to be applied in our own spiritual lives, and ends each chapter with a practical exercise to apply what is being learned.

This is a book for all who wish to understand the spirituality of the Sacred Heart, or have sought to understand the true place of our own hearts in Christian discipleship and ministry. No one will come away from this volume without learning something new about Christian faith, and with a challenge and inspiration to deepen their own faith and their response of their heart to God's love in Christ.

+ *Gregory Llanelwy*
Bishop of St Asaph
Bishop Visitor to the Sodality of Mary, Mother of Priests

Acknowledgements

Having long been drawn to the Hearts of Jesus and Mary I am grateful to Canterbury Press for publishing a book concerning a subject overlooked or dismissed by most non-Roman Catholics (and even some of those). At a time when parts of church and society seem riven by discord I hope this book, published during the 350th anniversary celebrations of the apparitions of the Sacred Heart to St Margaret-Mary Alacoque VHM, might be a reminder of what we're called to as Heart seeks to speak to hearts often deaf to Love's message.

I'm again indebted to Chris, my partner, whose loving heart generously made sure I had the space and time needed for writing, and grateful for the help given by Antonia Brotchie, the Revd Susanne Carlson, the Revd Mother Clare-Louise SLG, Ruth Cook, John Heath, Joanne McCrone, Sr Rosemary SLG, Sr Stephanie O.Carm., the Revd Ed Sniecienski and many others whose constructive criticisms, comments and insights have been so helpful. Thanks also to the Revd Steven Shakespeare, Professor of Continental Philosophy of Religion, Liverpool Hope University, for permission to reproduce his poem 'To the Heart', and to Katherine Bogner of www.looktohimandberadiant.com, for use of an image of the Immaculate Heart of Mary on page 28.

Finally, all I've written could be summed up in the simple motto of SS Francis de Sales and Jane Francis de Chantal: *Live Jesus*.

Introduction

'Home is where the heart is …'

'*… and my heart is anywhere you are*', crooned Elvis Presley in the 1962 film *Kid Galahad*. I was never a great fan of the 'King' but the words touched my 16-year-old heart, not least because they go on to declare that his home is anywhere his beloved is, which offers a profound expression of the Christian's relationship with Christ.

This is a book about two hearts, the Heart of Jesus and our own heart. Too often people dismiss the existence of God because it can't be 'proved'. But many scientists now believe that only the existence of 'Dark Matter' and 'Dark Energy', which also cannot be proved and don't follow the predicted rules of astrophysics, can account for some of the otherwise inexplicable mysteries of the galaxies. But for two thousand years millions of people have believed that faith in a God offers the way to a fullness of life that comes as they open their hearts to this Mystery. Jesus is concerned with changing our heart, refashioning it so it can love divinely and, as a foundation, affirmed the importance of the two great commandments: 'You shall love the Lord your God with all your heart, and with all your soul, and with all your mind … [and] your neighbour as yourself.' After his resurrection he underlined this when he asked Peter *three times*, 'Do you love me …?' His triple question probes the heart of one who, three times, had denied his Lord. How might we respond if Jesus asked that of us? If, as it pierces into the heart's depths, our honest reply is 'I don't know …', it's important not to let the passion of despair fill the heart, but to turn our gaze upon the Lord and say, with faith and trust, '… but help me to want to want to love you with every fibre of my being – and by all my words and deeds to love you "more than these"'. After all, the One we're called to love is Love, Life, Justice, Mercy and Wisdom realized in the Heart of Jesus.

Loving God

As a teenager I often fell in love and, as Valentine's Day came around each year, looked forward to receiving those anonymous cards with large, red hearts that weren't just signs of a blood-pumping muscle but assurances that *someone* out there loved me.

Those years were also a time of spiritual awakening, although the church I attended gave no impression that the heart might be of importance to faith. Christianity concerned worshipping God in church and how you lived, and while I was taught the importance of Holy Communion the Heart and Spirit animating that sacrament was never mentioned. So this book, as its title suggests, explores how giving attention to Jesus' (Sacred) Heart can assist in deepening our relationship with God. And in case some respond, 'But isn't that Roman Catholic?' we should remember that God's Heart is offered to all.

> I love you, O LORD, my strength,
> … my God, my rock in whom I take refuge.
> (Psalm 18.1)

I know certain of its images can seem overly sentimental and gruesome so, if that's your experience, be patient; take what's useful and place the rest where it could be considered later, for this divine Mystery has much to reveal. To develop a relationship with this Heart (which will be referred to with a capital H) means giving attention to the source of that love informing our faith while, conversely, doing so to those with corrupted hearts – not least of demagogues and dictators – is likely to blind us to the light of Christ.

Find the door of your heart and you will find the door to the kingdom of heaven. (St John Chrysostom, 347–407)

God's command to Moses, 'You shall love the LORD your God with all your heart, and with all your soul, and with all your might', is both a cause of joy and is what lies behind the great Song of Songs in the Hebrew scriptures. The often neglected, beautiful, erotic poem directing attention to the heart's desire for its Beloved is mirrored by Psalm 139 which recounts how the Beloved searches us out. But how can we love something we cannot see? Some maintain that only acts of service can fulfil this command and, although we can't love God if we hate others, we need to consider how service needs motivating by, and be an aspect of, our primary love of God. St Augustine of Hippo (354–430) pointed to this in his *Treatises on St John*: 'The love of God comes first in the order of command, but the love of neighbour first in the order of action' and Jesus re-affirmed that the love of God is the 'greatest and first commandment'. Why? Because it needs to motivate our heart: loving our neighbour might seem straightforward but that doesn't prevent us having other gods, be they politicians or presidents, ideologies, dogmas, nations, jobs – even families. And each has its dangers: if the heart isn't being converted by and to love, then whatever we do is open to corruption.

Western culture today can seem more interested in the external and active and be dismissive of God, but has our quest for 'head knowledge' caused us to overlook the need to cultivate 'heart wisdom'? They're not necessarily in conflict, but overemphasis on the former may provide us with many facts yet overlook that Holy Wisdom that was cultivated for millennia. We can have much 'knowledge', but lack the Wisdom coming from the incarnate Word speaking into the depths of our heart, something St Paul reminds us in the Letter to the Ephesians:

> *I pray that, according to the riches of his glory, [God] may grant that you may be strengthened in your inner being with power through his Spirit, and that Christ may dwell in your hearts through faith, as you are being rooted and grounded in love. I pray that you may have the power to comprehend, with all the saints, what is the breadth and length and height and depth, and to know the love of Christ that surpasses knowledge, so that you may be filled with all the fullness of God. (3.16–19)*

Heart and mind

The fourteenth-century author of *The Cloud of Unknowing* warned us that 'by love can [God] be gotten and holden but by thought, never'. It's not that the mind/brain isn't important, but it needs enfolding in the 'heart', our hidden unifying centre which, informed by the Spirit, directs the way we live while symbolizing the inner source of our emotions, feelings and passions – which can even cause our biological heart to beat faster.

> *Search me, O God, and know my heart;*
> *test me and know my thoughts.*
> *(Psalm 139.23)*

Spirit, mind and body are to be integrated, something most of us haven't achieved, leading St Theophan the Recluse (1815–94) to observe: 'All your inner disorder is due to the dislocation of your powers, the mind and heart each going their own way. You must unite the mind with the heart: then the tumult of your thoughts will cease, and you will acquire a rudder to guide the ship of your soul, a lever with which to put all your inner world in movement.'[1]

This points to our 'deep heart' where, as in the holy of holies in the Jerusalem Temple, Holy Wisdom abides, a wisdom inaccessible to our thinking minds. Denial of the inner, spiritual life carries great dangers as every therapist knows; it's not that we need to become introspective (although reflection is essential for maturing) nor be trapped in our inner world, but it's important to be aware of what happens in the heart and consider what Jesus meant by saying:

'The good person out of the good treasure of the heart produces good, and the evil person out of evil treasure produces evil; for it is out of the abundance of the heart that the mouth speaks.' (Luke 6.45)

As my faith developed I came to realize that God 'aims' at the heart, and whatever attractiveness we might have needs to concern our inner being. Excessive attention to physical appearance is less important: people may look on the outward, but 'the LORD looks on the heart' (1 Samuel 16.7, cf. 1 Peter 3.4). Beneath our veneer lies that which can reflect the wonder of Light, but has darker caverns harbouring the 'fallen angels' haunting and taunting us, those easily dismissed 'inciters of sin' animating us and wanting domination and control. So this book will consider those 'inner drivers' making us tick, in the place where that great laywoman St

---

1 https://www.stgeorgerosebay.org.au/wp-content/uploads/2019/01/Philokalia-13_-Mind-and-Heart.pdf (accessed 2.09.2024).

Catherine of Genoa (1447–1510) taught that the trinity of spirit, soul and body, guided by the Spirit, meet to dialogue.

Heart and heart

To 'put your whole heart' into something reflects the way Jesus' Heart was enfleshed by the incarnation revealing that love holds nothing back for the 'self' but gives all to the other. So when someone 'gives' you their heart they're entrusting their most precious gift to you, one to be treated with the utmost respect, care and thanksgiving.

> The heart has its reasons which reason knows
>   nothing of ...
> We know the truth not only by the reason,
>   but by the heart.
> (Blaise Pascal, 1623–62, Pensées)

The Hindu mystic Swami Krishnananda (1922–2001), writes: 'If only one were to dive into the ocean of one's own heart, one would see there everything that one cannot even dream of in one's mind' (The Chandogya Upanishad, Ch. 4, Sec. 3).

Orthodox and Reformed

Although Orthodox Christians haven't developed devotion to the Sacred Heart, they have, like many non-Christian religions, a profound spirituality of the heart expressed by the Jesus Prayer – 'Lord Jesus Christ, Son of God; have mercy on me, a sinner' – that rhythmic prayer that descends from the lips into the heart.

Heart-centred devotion flourished in England until the Reformation, reappearing on 23 May 1738, when John Wesley's heart was suddenly 'warmed' on hearing Luther's description of the change God works in the heart through faith in Christ. Luther chose as his seal a black cross placed in a red heart set in a white rose, and there's evidence Wesley was drawn to devotion to the Heart of Jesus, not least because he arranged for the reprint of the book by seventeenth-century English Puritan Thomas Goodwin: *The Heart of Christ in Heaven towards Sinners on Earth.* All this formed part of the background to the consequent Evangelical Revival.

Human growth

Nowadays, from heart emoji's and 'finger-hearts' made by linking thumbs and forefingers to the way someone 'wears their heart on their sleeve', the heart is the universal symbol of love. The Sacred Heart is even a popular tattoo, considered by some to symbolize rebirth from a chaotic time in their lives and reminding them of the importance of compassion towards others.

In an era encouraging us to stimulate our mind, practise competitive sports (producing winners – and losers) with the aim of being 'successful', some can overlook the importance of attending to their inner life. But, as our ancestors knew, to ignore that leaves a person vulnerable to gods who would mislead us. Yet neither wealth, success nor celebrity can fulfil the heart's deepest needs, although their appeal can blind us to the heart of Christian faith which, long before mindfulness became popular, offers the means to encounter the centre of our being. For society to ignore religion because, like the arts, it's considered uneconomic, unnecessary – or unfashionable, even dangerous – damages development of the whole person, potentially leading to children growing into adults out of touch with themselves, a situation compounded if they encounter churches neglectful of the inner life. Rather than turning to God when occasion demands, or even once a week, it's God's Heart that needs to animate our lives – Jesus, may all that is you flow into me. More than simply an object of pious devotion, being human involves realizing and responding to this sacred heartbeat.

Within these pages ...

... we'll explore how devotion to the Sacred Heart, rooted in scripture, was understood to be of importance from the early Christian era, going on to speak to the needs of medieval Europe. And because the heart is central to many faiths, I've used writings from them which illustrate that as people come closer to God what they experience can be strikingly similar – and any unattributed prayers you'll find in these pages are one's I've created. We'll also consider why Jesus' Beatitude 'Blessed are the pure in heart ...' is of such importance, look at the Heart's relationship with the Religious Life, priesthood and Eucharist, and end each chapter with spiritual exercises and questions for consideration. Finally, because he who is Son of the Father is also the Word by which creation came into being, there's a chapter on the cosmic Heart.

The Heart of Jesus is
the ultimate symbol of God's mercy.
But it is not an imaginary symbol;
it is a real symbol which represents the centre,
the source from which salvation flowed
for all of humanity.
(Pope Francis)

The image of the Sacred Heart

I was once given a large, old, dirty statue of the Sacred Heart much of whose paint had flaked off. Few would have given it a second glance but I found a devout painter who refreshed the red robe, gave it back a creamy-white tunic and refreshed the hand pointing to its restored golden Heart. But my religious community didn't want it so I gave it to the church where, eventually, I served; it looked at home on a neo-gothic window ledge and I hope it's still happy there.

All art is subjective. Some consider depictions of the Sacred Heart as saccharine or bloodthirsty and see Valentine's hearts as a more appropriate image for love. Yet images of the Sacred Heart aren't meant to appeal to sentimentality and certainly not any sadistic streak but to stimulate awareness of, and for, Christ, and this particular image invites us to internalize our faith. Evelyn Underhill (1875–1941), the great Anglican writer on spiritual matters, described it as 'a pictured expression of one of the deepest intuitions of the human soul caught up into the contemplation of God's love' (*Mysticism*, 1995, p. 267).

Art can provide a doorway that the rational mind cannot enter: 'It is only with the heart that one can see rightly; what is essential is invisible to the eye,' said the 'Little Prince' in Antoine de Saint-Exupéry's book of that name. This 'seeing' is similar to the visions of mystics or what can be revealed in dreams: it isn't dependent on bodily sight, and shows an unfathomable ocean of love, the power of which can even draw Christ's Heart from his body. This is illustrated by the story of the boy who, shown a depiction of Jesus holding out a flaming Heart, was asked why and tentatively responded: 'Because he loves us so much, he couldn't keep it in?' So, let's take a closer look …

The enlightening flames

This Heart confronts us with the truth that Valentine's cards
don't declare – God's love is realized through self-sacrifice
– the self-sacrifice of a Son on the fiery altar of the cross.
Here are the flames Moses saw in the burning bush, forming the fiery column of the Divine presence which guided
the Israelites during desert nights. It enflamed the disciples'
hearts on the road to Emmaus, settled on them at Pentecost
and was experienced by Paul on the Damascus road. They are
the Light that, at the end of time, will replace that of sun and
moon because the Lamb – Jesus – is its transfiguring source.

> *Come, Holy Spirit, fill the hearts of your faithful*
> *and enkindle in them the fire of your love.*
> (Common Worship, Daily Prayer)

The cross

Although the cross dwarfed Jesus, here it is his Heart which dwarfs the cross. It's a powerful expression of the crucifixion as the sign of God's endless love and another image of the column accompanying the Israelites through their daytime wilderness wanderings.

It is this sign of suffering love we're to contemplate and assimilate: Jesus' Heart, aflame with love, was also pierced, bled and broken on the cross and it needs to touch our hearts: it is the reality of our love-embodied God which the world needs to know.

The bloody wound

The wound in Christ's side from which flowed blood and water, fountain of the church's sacramental life, reveals how much Jesus suffered for love of us. Until anaesthetics were available, pain was a common factor in people's lives – the great, graphic sixteenth-century Isenheim altarpiece was created for the city's plague hospital of St Antony to remind patients that God-in-Christ shared their suffering. This gaping wound also reveals the entrance to his Heart just as the Temple's torn curtain revealed God's presence in the holy of holies.

The crown of thorns

While the scriptures tell of Jesus being crowned with thorns, here they are shown encircling his Heart. This seems another 'wounding' pointing to how the Passion caused the crucifixion of Christ's heart; yet this crown will also be a symbol of victory.

Reflection

- 'You shall love the Lord your God ...' What might that mean for you?
- What might be off-putting about loving God?
- How does your church help you to deepen that love?

Exercise

Read Luke 1.39–56.

Set an alarm for 5–10 minutes. Sit quietly on a supportive chair, gently direct your attention into the 'cavern of the heart'. Make the sign of the cross and, breathing deeply into your heart, inhale the words, 'Remove my heart of stone', and exhale, 'Give me a heart of flesh'. Let go of distractions, allow the prayer to sink into your heart and, at the end, give thanks.

The Heart of the Trinity

Of the Father's heart begotten,
Ere the world from chaos rose,
He is Alpha, from that Fountain
All that is and hath been flows;
He is Omega, of all things,
Yet to come the mystic Close,
Evermore and evermore.

This Christmas hymn has long touched me. Set to a haunting tenth-century plainsong melody it's based on a poem by Aurelius Prudentius Clemens (348–c.413) which refers to a verse from John's Gospel (1.18), and while it's sometimes translated, 'Of the Father's *love* begotten', the Latin word used by Clemens, *corde*, means 'heart'.

When you love you should not say, 'God is in my heart,'
but rather, 'I am in the heart of God.'
(Khalil Gibran, 1863–1931, The Prophet)

The God who draws us

As a child I assumed 'God' must be a great 'sky father' who controlled everything, but eventually came to realize this isn't what the church teaches. Rather than a physical 'being' encountered through our outward senses this Mystery is knowable, in the words of the great pastor of the Reformation era St Francis de Sales (1567–1622), as *'cor ad cor loquitor'* – 'heart to heart speaks' (*Treatise on the Love of God*, Ch. 1) which, as anyone becomes aware of a certain drawing in the heart, can move them to want to 'go deeper'. But if faith is nurtured in a tradition emphasizing stringent and narrow guidelines any sense of wanting to reach beyond those can be extremely uncomfortable and people may find their fellow Christians, even their ministers, warning them against this desire. But God, as the great eleventh-century Archbishop of Canterbury St Anselm declared, is 'greater than which we can conceive' and wants everyone to know more of the depths of Love.

A community of love

So Christianity declares that God isn't a remote, solitary Being, but a wonderful Mystery named as Father/Creator, Son/Redeemer, Holy Spirit/Sanctifier whom Nicholas of Cusa (1401–64) described as an 'Eternal Circle from Goodness through Goodness to Goodness ... everything which is'. These three equal 'Persons' exist in an eternal 'dance' of love known as *perichoresis*, into which we're to be gathered – a movement recognized through the silence of the heart. Christopher Harvey (1587–1663), the poet-son of Puritan parents, sought to express this in 'The School of the Heart':

> *The whole round world is not enough to fill*
> *The heart's three corners, but it craveth still;*
> *None but the Trinity, who made it, can*
> *Suffice the vast triangulated heart of man.*

This is similar to a Sufi teaching (*Hadith Qudsi*) about God: '[I am] a hidden Treasure that desired to be known. So I manifested all creation to reveal the essence of the deep secret knowing of Myself.' The Protestant mystic, Jacob Böehme (1575–1624), offers this word-picture: 'If you conceive a small minute circle, as small as a grain of mustard seed, yet the Heart of God is wholly and perfectly therein: and if thou art born in God, then there is in thyself (in the circle of thy life) the whole Heart of God undivided' (Underhill, *Mysticism*, p. 100). It is this which the church names the Trinity.

Christianity, along with Judaism and Islam, is a 'Religion of the Book', but differs from them in believing that one 'Word' is more important than the rest, a Word – Jesus – that dwelt among us. This 'Word' took flesh from a Woman, spoke of God as his Father, taught us to pray to him and, in the famous Parable of the Prodigal/Two Sons, revealed that God's Heart has an overwhelming, compassionate longing for us. It was from this Heart that that Love flowed which, alone, can overcome the evil present in our world (Genesis 6.12). Yet a society that has abandoned its Christian roots will have lost such an awareness.

Today many who have nothing to do with the church might claim that it's 'love' that gives meaning to life – and it is, as one film declared, a 'many-splendored thing' as well as being the essence of our faith. However, while we say 'God is love' we don't affirm that love is God because that limits the Divine. If we ignore *that* Mystery and everything Christianity teaches about how to nurture love, guard the heart and avoid its corruption then it's easy for the heart to be attracted by lesser, misleading gods. Easy to become fragmented head/heart people living in an equally fragmented world; easy to confuse 'heart' and 'spirit(uality)' with warm, fuzzy, slightly unearthly feelings while considering that the 'head' must dominate.

This 'drawing' into God's depths is the work of the Holy Spirit, that Holy Wisdom, Sophia, coming from the Most High, speaking into the heart and pervading the universe. She cannot be contained in the Heart of the Trinity but spills out, gathering all into that sacred and mysterious Trinitarian 'dance' of love, that dynamic 'Oneness of Being' Jesus wants the world to experience (John 17.23); that Love which, as Dante observed, 'moves the sun and the other stars' (*Paradiso XXXIII*). This is the Love that enabled Jesus to affirm, 'the Father and I are one' (John 10.30), and is what every Christian is to set their heart upon, for it is when we love that we are most human *and* divine: conversely, when we hate we emit the *in*human stench of corruption.

Yet unless we learn to love the Beloved we can become satisfied with less – as advertisers know – and never grow into the fullness of that Love found in the Sacred Heart. This is why the church and world need those consecrated to the contemplative life; those whose hearts are set on this Love and whose lives are given to that Love, for they can reveal vital insights about life's journey: while faith needs to informs us, love must inspire us.

Heart in the Hebrew scriptures

Although some may not realize the importance of the heart to belief it's referred to many, many times in the Hebrew scriptures. There 'heart' is understood as providing access to the deepest reality of who we are, the place where we establish our identity, the seat of our personal trinity of body, soul and spirit; of mind (understanding), memory (brain) and will (intentions) – helping us make wise choices. Moses recalled the Israelites to its importance after encountering God (Yahweh) on Mount Sinai:

Hear, O Israel: The LORD *is our God, the* LORD *alone. You shall love the* LORD *your God with all your heart, and with all your soul, and with all your might. Keep these words that I am commanding you today in your heart. Recite them to your children and talk about them*

*when you are at home and when you are away, when you
lie down and when you rise. (Deuteronomy 6.4–7)*

This command can be read as a threat – 'You shall … *or
else!*', but also as a promise – 'You *shall* … go to the ball.' It
concerns putting us in a right relationship with that Trinity of
Love which is what every church exists to declare and is also
a message for nations, for our faith can never be individual-
istic. By the power of the Holy Spirit that Love flowed into
the world from the Father's Heart, affirming that 'eternal life'
is gained by St Thérèse of Lisieux's 'Little Way' of loving God
and neighbour.

A heart united with God

Until a hundred years ago most people would have heard of the
primacy of loving God, but now? Is love of God simply about
serving others? Or coming to 'fullness of life'?' Does it mean
going to church – and is that, as some claim, for reassurance,
companionship or experiencing an adrenaline rush through
worship? And when, and if, that no longer satisfies or is possible – when 'church' gets 'boring', what then …?

Whatever we love has power to inform us, so it would seem
of fundamental importance that we give primary attention to
the source and essence of Love. Secular education will, hopefully, have left its mark on us, but if the church fails to teach
and explain *this* message where will the lesson be learnt?
Of course our love can never be more than an obscured
reflection of God's, whose love is beyond our wildest dreams.
But if human love can be as strong and beautiful as some
experience, the source of Love must be greater than the
greatest love we can know. This is the concern of the Song
of Songs (of Solomon): our humanity will never be fulfilled
until our heart is united with the Heart of that Love which
would inspire ours. It is that which formed us – and animates

creation – and as the church seeks to connect with people she needs to remember that her primary purpose is to be what she is – not an organization, but the mystical Body of Christ whose Heart is at-one with God.

> *My child, give me your heart,*
> *and let your eyes observe my ways.*
> *(Proverbs 23.26)*

Temple, heart and purity

It was Isaiah who prophesied that the Lord would dwell in the hearts of those who are 'contrite and humble in spirit' (57.15), using the metaphor of marriage to express God's relationship with Israel. The Jerusalem Temple, parts of which were open to believer and unbeliever alike, was the sacrament of that relationship although its heart, its most holy of holies, was curtained off and only accessible to the purified High Priest.

While God's passionate desire for us was located in that Most Holy Place, the good inclinations in ours can become degraded. This led Jeremiah to acknowledge that the heart is 'devious above all else; it is perverse – who can understand it? I the LORD test the mind and search the heart' (17.9–10). So Ezekiel prophesied that people needed a 'change of heart' because theirs had turned to stone which God could replace with a 'heart of flesh' (36.26). Here we touch that truth the church has a primary responsibility to proclaim: that in spite of any 'advances' we may make, if we don't guard the heart then humanity is in danger of corruption. But the Sacred Heart is uncorrupted, for God's heart is pure – it is, as the *Song of Manasseh* declares, 'full of compassion and mercy and love' (*Common Worship*, Church of England).

Such understanding might seem counter-cultural, but our faith challenges any belief system dominated by the intellect *or* emotions; by success or winners and losers, the one rewarded and the other thrown out. And although success is appealing it can demand achievement, fear, failure, promote competitiveness and be tempted by the lure of pride and desire for domination – a toxic mix, especially when religion is added, which is why the Sacred Heart, emblazoned with symbols of the Crucified, offers a necessarily counter-cultural image. The way to this 'temple' isn't through willpower but by becoming familiar with that still space within us; by nurturing the virtues and letting that voice which called Jesus 'beloved Son' speak into our heart.

> *As we rejoice in the gift of this new day,*
> *so may the light of your presence, O God,*
> *set our hearts on fire with love for you;*
> *now and for ever. Amen.*
> (Common Worship, Morning Prayer)

THE LOVE OF THE HEART OF JESUS

> *Whoever has Jesus in his heart,*
> *will soon have him in his external actions.*
> *(St Francis de Sales, Introduction to the Devout Life,*
> *p. 170)*

Love, of course, isn't God, but we can find its perfect example in Christ, the God-man: there's something of the divine in everyone, a spark of that Love which mystics know and, when fanned, burns brightly, for:

> *From love in Love the leaping flame of love is spread*
> *For none can love except by Love possessed.*
> (Fr Gilbert Shaw, A Pilgrim's Book of Prayers, *p. 60*)

This is the love found in the Heart of Jesus, a love that inspired St Francis of Assisi (1182–1226) in his night-long prayer, *'Deus meus et omnia'* (My God and all): for Francis knew himself a beloved sinner. Such awareness has led people to die for Christ and still inspires Christians to live out their baptismal consecration to God, a consecration that acknowledges that the heart is a battleground between forces of darkness and light while affirming the ultimate triumph of the latter. Some consider that the heart of Christian faith concerns discerning – sifting – the various calls aimed at our heart until we sense from where they come and how best to respond, and it's this which St Ignatius Loyola (1491–1556) writes about with such wisdom in his *Spiritual Exercises*.

The Word in the heart

Some find their heart's set ablaze after a 'Damascus conversion' (Acts 9), but faith's journey can begin with rather hazy feelings about God. It took me many years to realize the importance of Jesus or the Holy Spirit – somehow I'd missed out on them at Sunday School – and when I pondered simple questions like 'What's the meaning of life?' I decided that if God 'existed' then, as saints declare, there's nothing of greater importance on which to set the heart. So I began to reflect on why I went to church … was it simply a matter of feeling better afterwards and learning useful lessons? I felt there had to be … more … and then I discovered Paul's words to the Ephesians about our need to 'know' Christ in the depths of our heart (3.16f.). Gradually 'church' became not just a building or even people, but Christ's mystical Body, and statements like 'God's love has been poured into our hearts through the Holy Spirit that has been given to us' (Romans 5.5) resonated.

I realized another dimension to life and wanted to know more. The heart seemed to offer a doorway into a great

Mystery and I began to realize life isn't meant to be a quest for riches or power nor an aimless wandering but a pilgrimage – a marathon not a sprint – from the darkness of the womb to that of the tomb, with the eye of the heart always set on Jesus. I sensed a voice calling 'seek me' and began to realize that the heart is created for union, human and divine, with the Sacred Heart as the 'bridge' between them. It's the image of what ours *can* become, for we're fully human as we enter into the life of the God-man, Jesus. Even if you've had a sudden conversion, ongoing faith requires nurturing a loving heart – love of Love, love of the other, love of self – else it can become heart-less. 'Your relationship with your heart is your relationship with Me,' affirmed a Sufi teacher (*The Knowing Heart*, p. 260).

CHRIST, THE IMAGE OF GOD

The invisible things of God have been made visible.
(John of Damascus, c.675–749, Defence Against Those
Who Oppose Images)

In the opening chapter of Genesis we read God saying: 'Let us make humankind in our image, according to our likeness.' Apart from that one little word, 'us/our', suggestive of the way 'God' isn't a solo act, it doesn't say that *we*, humankind, are the image of God – that's Christ, the *imago Dei* – but 'in'. That doesn't mean Jesus physically resembles God but that we have the *capacity* to reflect his Hearts-likeness as St Gregory of Nyssa (c.335–95) expressed in his profound *Commentary on the Song of Songs* (II, PG 44, 805d):

The sky was not made in God's image, nor the moon, nor the sun, nor the beauty of the stars, nor other things which appear in creation. Only you (human soul) were made to be the image of nature that surpasses every intellect, likeness of incorruptible beauty, mark of true divinity, vessel of blessed life, image of true light, that when you look upon it you become what He is, because through the reflected ray coming from your purity you imitate He who shines within you. Nothing that exists can measure up to your greatness.

This affirms our creation in God's 'likeness'; and when that likeness recognizes the same in Christ – the 'new man', the 'new Adam' – it is either attracted or repelled for it cannot bear to see what it could become until such time as it loses its shame and fear through Love's awakening attraction. This is what causes our restlessness as Augustine said in his *Confessions*.

Images and scripture

Images also concern what the psychologist Carl Jung called 'archetypes', primal symbols such as birth and death, floods, caves, etc. connecting with our 'collective unconscious'. Images of the heart seem to fit this category as they are a universal symbol of love and intimacy communicating without use of words (i.e. metaphorically). In a letter to one of his patients in 1916 Jung maintained: 'your vision will become clear only when you can look into your own heart. ... *Who looks outside dreams; who looks inside awakes.*'

However, because they can also mislead, God commanded Moses not to make any 'image or likeness of anything in heaven' (Exodus 20.4f.). Yet when God provided an image of God's-self (Jesus) Christians began to believe it right – and proper – to portray that image until some declared them idolatrous and icons were destroyed (*First Iconoclasm*, c.730–87). Later St John of Damascus (675/6–749) defended their use in these important words: 'I do not worship matter, I worship the God of matter, who became matter for my sake and deigned to inhabit matter, who worked out my salvation through matter. I will not cease from honouring that matter which works for my salvation. I venerate it, though not as God.'

But because worship is a response of the heart to what it both loves and desires, the later English Reformers wanted to restrict it to God alone and so stated that: 'The ... worshipping and adoration as well of images ... is a fond thing vainly invented' (Church of England, *Article* 22), and although this doesn't say they *can't* be used it led to their destruction. People were again denied opportunity to encounter the deeper levels of spiritual awareness images can enable while reflecting an ancient heresy (Manichaeism) that condemned the physical body as evil. Forbidding sacred images might have also aided the loss of awareness of our 'inner eye', making it hard for some to recognize the hidden, darker forces in our world.

But it's not merely images that can become idols. Verses of scripture can be if used in ways that ignore respected biblical criticism; religious faith can also be idolatrous when equated with nationhood, allowing the emotive elements in religion to pervert Christ's gospel. All this feeds exclusivity, fear and judgementalism while overlooking our primary need to nurture a loving heart for God to mould.

In churches where images are found it's important to consider *why* they're there. In some places they seem to mark a spot where, for example, a candle could simply be lit, but if we stopped and gazed upon the image *itself* or taught children that, like pictures of loved ones, it offered a means of seeing beyond into the reality it points to then the image could, again, work on our subconscious. We might even find that meditating on the Sacred Heart helped connect with the Mystery within our own.

Kissing images, like bowing to an altar, reverencing the Blessed Sacrament and devotions such as the rosary, the Jesus Prayer or making the Stations of the Cross can personalize faith by connecting the devotion with the heart. We know the importance of being 'devoted' to a life-partner, but do we realize the importance of devotion to Jesus and the saints? To enter a church where people are engaged in spiritual practices communicates much. In the one I normally attend there's a large, ancient icon of the Theotokos, the God-bearer (Mary), before which I pray after receiving the Holy Communion and, as I gaze upon her whose heart nurtured Christ, I find myself wanting to touch – kiss – the image but, for fear of standing out, feel unable to do so. Yet what might be awoken in *me* if I sought that encounter with the Holy Child ... with Mary?

Sacred images are sacramental – outward and visible manifestations of what is inward and invisible – and devotion to them can link us to the mystery they portray. Gazing upon them can inform the heart more powerfully than words, and part of the importance of images of the Sacred Heart is that they can connect with believer and unbeliever alike.

'VIVE JESUS!' – *LIVE JESUS!*

Since the heart is the source of actions,
as the heart is, so they are. ...
I have desired above all things
to engrave and inscribe this
holy and sacred word upon your heart, Vive Jesus!
(Francis de Sales, Introduction to the Devout Life, *III, Ch. 23)*

This Heart beats to enliven the Body to which we belong. It is the focus of the Old and New Covenant, a crucible of love which, according to scripture, is open to all (Mark 16.15), its presence blessing those excluded by Jesus' fellow Jews (Luke 5.29f.). It is of such importance that he, lovingly, invited one young man to examine how much he would give up to have this treasure (Mark 10). That encounter shows how love animated Jesus' Heart and how he longs for us to join him in loving as he loves, his greatest condemnation reserved for those who taught otherwise (Matthew 23). Francis de Sales accepted this invitation – hence his motto, '*Vive Jesus!*' – and wrote about it in a number of important books. One of them, *Introduction to the Devout Life*, has been immensely helpful to Christians down the ages because its profoundly evangelical spirituality concerns a simple means to live in union with the Lord's will:

- Encouraging people to turn their heart to Jesus' Heart through prayer and meditation.
- Revealing this Heart through simple acts of kindness.
- Proclaiming our faith 'heart to heart'.
- Reflecting daily on how we are living this love and making regular use of the confessional.

'As soon as we give some attention to God', de Sales wrote, 'we feel a certain sweet emotion within our heart. This shows that God is God of the human heart ... we are created in the image and likeness of God, what does this mean if not that we have the greatest likeness with God' (*Treatise on the Love of God*, 1.15).

Knowing we're called to live by way of faith, hope and love and believing God will work with us when we're seeking to do the Divine will – as Mary did – Francis believed God will make it clear if we follow a wrong path. He saw Jesus' call to holiness as universal, something recalled by Pope Francis in his 2018 encyclical, *Gaudete et Exsultate*: 'We are all called to be holy by living our lives with love and by bearing witness in everything we do, wherever we find ourselves.'

Love Jesus

In his book *The Four Loves*, C. S. Lewis (1898–1963) described different types of love: affection, friendship, romantic/erotic and agape/charity, seeing the latter as selfless love – the greatest love. But it needed to be enfleshed lest it become mere sentimentality, so to recognize Divine Love we need to consider how Jesus lived and ask ourselves: 'Do I love as he did ...? Do I want/seek to ...?' Mystics like de Sales – those who lovingly have their hearts set on God – reveal the fundamental question for us, the one Jesus posed to Peter, is simply: 'Do I love Jesus?' (John 21.15). To listen deeply to that question can encourage us to seek a greater love in which our heart can delight until we can say, with our whole heart, 'Yes, Lord; you know I love you.'

> *I was daily his delight,*
> * rejoicing before him always,*
> *rejoicing in his inhabited world*
> * and delighting in the human race.*
> *(Proverbs 8.30–31)*

Unfortunately the doctrines and behaviour of some Christians obscure this, giving the impression that turning to Jesus makes you irrational, judgemental and fanatical. But gazing upon the Sacred Heart will reveal how much Jesus simply loves us because, as many have noted, God can do no other. His gaze will help us see ourselves as we are; we'll begin to recognize what we're called to become and a desire will gradually awaken within the heart to grow 'to the measure of the full stature of Christ' (Ephesians 4.13). And because of the importance of this the church needs to help people encounter and respond to these movements – to nurture the *imago* seeking to be formed in the heart. (Galatians 4.19).

Growing in Christ's image

That *imago*, the fruit of Mary's womb, is seen by some as simply a good person. Others want to serve Jesus and his Reign, but forget (or aren't aware) that needs doing from a primary – deepening – relationship with him. The 'doing-bit' can be obvious – caring, evangelizing, offering liturgies, etc. – but it's easy to forget that we need to nurture a heart-centred relationship with Christ. Whatever else we spend time on we need to 'waste' time on him, letting ourselves be enfolded in his Heart as we offer him our own. This often involves a threefold faith development:

- *Initially exciting but rootless,* Jesus is seen as a wonderful, heroic leader.
- *Settling into a way* of following him, but eventually losing commitment because the process is slow, profound questions aren't explored.
- *Digging deeper* into a less feelings-driven relationship, but being drawn by and committed to Love regardless of how we feel or of the darkness that comes as the seed of faith takes root in our heart.

Awake, O my soul. How long will you remain asleep?
Beyond the sky there is a King who wishes to possess you;
He loves you immeasurably, with all His Heart.
He loves you with so much kindness and faithfulness
that He left His kingdom and humbled Himself for you,
permitting Himself to be bound like a criminal
in order to find you.
(St Gertrude of Helfta, Gertrude the Great, *1256–1302)*

Reflections

- There's a theme in the Hebrew scriptures that God's Heart has a primary concern for Israel and fights their enemies, but other understandings are also present. Read Micah 6.8 and consider how this might challenge a tribal people. How might the notion of the Lord being a tribal god affect the heart of families, churches, nations?
- How do images connect with us and why (and how) might the church make use of them?
- What aspects of the Sacred Heart might you need to nurture?
- There are times in the Gospels when Jesus' Heart is revealed. Matthew 26.38f. speaks of it 'nearly breaking' (Revised English Bible) – what do you think Jesus meant?

Practical exercise

If your church is able, arrange for a Shrine of the Sacred Heart, with appropriate description, to be erected which would be visible to passers-by.

SH.1: A PRAYER PRACTICE

(*Most prayer-practices and other resources are available to download.*[1])

This exercise could take place in the context of a Quiet Day etc., and requires a table around which people can walk. Scatter on it cards bearing various images of the Sacred/Compassionate Heart – examples can be found online.

Explain that people will be invited to view images representing the Heart of Jesus. Offer an initial prayer and time of stillness, then encourage them to spend a few minutes walking around the table gazing at the pictures (not *thinking* about them) until one catches their attention. Having picked it up they return to their chair and, after a brief centring exercise, ask them to take a 'long, loving look' at their image, noticing its colour, texture, facets, etc. 'What touches/moves you? Speaks into your heart?' Spend ten minutes silently focusing on the image after which each person is invited (not required) to share with the group the effect the image had on them. The exercise ends in prayer[2] and, ideally, people take their card home.

---

1 https://johnfrancisfriendship.co.uk/sacred-hearts

2 After further silence you could invite them to consider Jesus looking at them and saying: 'I see your struggles and my Heart goes out to you! But gently turn your heart to me and say: "Jesus, I love and trust you ..." Then seek to walk in my ways and let yourself rest in my heart.'

2

Sacred Hearts

'Where your treasure is,
there will your heart be also.'
(Matthew 6.21)

Christianity is the faith of a Word uttered by the mouth of God whose voice, as Elijah discovered, is heard in silence. Our culture tends to be swamped by words – printed, spoken, sung; politely, aggressively, deceitfully, lovingly – but only if they're allowed to enter the heart through its silent portal can words take root and have a powerful effect. If hearts have become corrupted then they will seek to dominate and, if allowed to do so, will wreak immense damage.

DEVELOPMENT OF HEART-CENTRED SPIRITUALITY

... it is in the Heart of Jesus, Jesus as He is in His Glory, that we find set before us the vision of the Life and Love of God ... there is no short-cut to this intimacy with the sacred Heart ... It is here in this kind of intimacy with the Heart of Jesus, this most holy state where the Precious Blood does its most perfect work ... that there

is found that Christ-like perception of the needs and sorrows of the world which He has ransomed, and of the character and power of the Love of God to Whom we are redeemed. (Fr Lucius Cary SSJE, 1866–1950, Anima Christi Retreat, 1932)

Fr Cary was a member of the Anglican Society of St John the Evangelist, the 'beloved disciple' who opens his Gospel with a long meditation on the Word made flesh, going on to reveal the intimacy with which it encounters the heart. John described Jesus being moved to tears at the death of a close friend, and the intimate relationship between him and John was pointedly revealed at the Last Supper when John 'reclined', or rested, his head on Jesus' 'breast' (13.23, King James Version), an attitude that led to the idea that John heard the 'heartbeat of God'.

> *Within my flowering breast*
> *Which only for himself entire I save*
> *He sank into his rest*
> *And all my gifts I gave*
> *Lulled by the airs with which the cedars wave.*
> (St John of the Cross OCD, 1542–91)

Origins

As early as the beginning of the second-century, Justin Martyr, referring to John 7.37f., wrote: 'We the Christians are the true Israel which springs from Christ, for we are carved out of his heart as from a rock' (*Dialogue with the Jew Trypho*).

By the end of that century St Irenaeus, in *Adversus Haereses*, pointed out that the church is meant to be 'the fountain of the living water that flows to us from the Heart of Christ'. A hundred years later Christian devotion included pausing at the 'third hour' (Terce – 3pm) to recall Jesus' death and the piercing of his crucified side by a soldier's spear. This 'piercing' was seen to correspond with the opening in Adam's side through which God formed Eve, the mother of all the living and from this wound the new Adam, Christ, the church – our new Mother – was understood to have 'emerged'. This wound was the doorway giving access to his Heart, the 'cleft' where Moses was placed as God passed by (Exodus 33.22):

> *'O my dove, in the clefts of the rock,*
> *in the covert of the cliff,*
> *let me see your face,*
> *let me hear your voice ...'*
> *(Song of Songs 2.14)*

Augustine of Hippo in north Africa, whose monastic Rule informed the founder/resses of many Anglican Religious Orders, wrote that 'The house of my soul is narrow; do Thou enter in and enlarge it! It is ruinous, do Thou repair it' (*Confessions, 5*). He is often depicted holding a flaming heart pierced by an arrow symbolizing the way, at his conversion, his own burst into flame with the love of God who calls us to growth in faith, hope and love. 'You have pierced our hearts,' he wrote, 'with the arrow of your love, and our minds were pierced with the arrows of your words' (*Confessions 9, 2*). The image also symbolizes his love for his brothers and sisters leading to that famous saying: 'You have made us for Yourself, O Lord, and our heart is restless until it rests in You' (*Confessions, 1.1*).

The Cistercians, a reform of the Benedictine Order, were profoundly affected by this devotion. St Bernard of Clairvaux

OCist. (1090–1153) said in a sermon: 'Through these sacred wounds we can see the secret of his Heart, the great mystery of love, the sincerity of his mercy with which he visited us from on high.' Another member of the Order, William of St Thierry (c.1080–1148), wrote in *On Contemplating God*: 'I want to see and touch the whole of him and – what is more – to approach the most holy wound in his side, the portal of the ark that is there made, and ... wholly enter into Jesus' very heart, into the holy of holies, the ark of the covenant.' Finally, St Aelred of Rievaulx (1110–67) wrote that the highest kind of friendship, that friendship that God invites us into, is a selfless communion of hearts (*Spiritual Friendship*, 1.45).

Middle Ages: Sacred wounds

Later, as plagues ravaged Europe, Christ's suffering humanity became a focus of devotion. People turned to his Heart for comfort, something seen in the life of Francis of Assisi who wrote:

> *May the power of your love, Lord Christ,*
> *fiery and sweet as honey,*
> *so absorb our hearts*
> *as to withdraw them from all that is under heaven.*
> *Grant that we may be ready*
> *to die for love of your love,*
> *as you died for love of our love.*
> (The Absorbeat)

Shortly after Francis' death St Bonaventure OFM (1221–74) wrote in *The Tree of Life*: 'Who will not love that Heart so deeply wounded? ... Who will not return love to One who so loved us? Who will not embrace a Spouse so chaste? Certainly the soul loves You in return, O Lord, who, knowing itself to be wounded by Your love, cries to You: "Your charity has wounded me!" We too, pilgrims in the flesh, love as much as we can, and embrace the One who was wounded for us, whose hands, feet, side, and Heart were pierced. Let us love and pray: O Jesus, deign to bind our hearts, still so hard and unrepentant, with the chain of Your love and wound them with its dart.'

Let us then bear in mind, Christian souls, the very great love Jesus has shown towards us by allowing His Side to be opened wide in order that we might have easy access to His Heart. Let us hasten to enter into the Heart of Jesus, bringing there all our love, and uniting it to His Divine love. (Ludolph of Saxony OCarth, c.1295–1378)

All five wounds, emblazoned on the Jerusalem Cross, came to be revered together with devotion to the instruments of Christ's Passion. His blood was venerated, especially at Hailes, Gloucestershire as Geoffrey Chaucer (c.1340–1400) mentions in *The Pardoner's Tale*, forming with those Five Wounds, an extremely popular 'affective' devotion (devotion stimulated by the feelings). At about the same time Julian of Norwich wrote in *Revelations of Divine Love*: 'Then with a glad expression our Lord looked into his side and gazed, rejoicing and with his dear gaze he led his creature's understanding through the same wound into his side within. And then he revealed a beautiful and delightful place, large enough for all mankind that shall be saved to rest there in peace and in love' (Ch. 24). Such devotion might no longer be as popular, but it spoke to people during times of great suffering and informed later Evangelical piety:

Jesu, grant me this, I pray,
ever in thy heart to stay;
let me evermore abide
hidden in thy wounded side.
(Author unknown, before 18th century)

NUPTIAL MYSTICISM

'Your Maker is your husband.' (Isaiah 54.5)

In the same century as Julian a movement developed, mostly in the Low Countries, of laywomen practising 'spiritual marriage'. Jesus was their joy, their love and the one with whom they sought an ever-deepening union, their heart being a 'bridal chamber' where, as a 'Spouse of Christ', they could express intense intimacy with him. Some men also practised this devotion and such an alternative expression of marriage might have something to say in today's debates about the subject. When St Margaret-Mary Alacoque (1647–90) received an apparition of the Sacred Heart surmounted by the cross covered in flames, Jesus told her that this was the 'bed of my spouse to consummate my love'.

> *I slept, but my heart was awake.*
> *Listen! my beloved is knocking.*
> *'Open to me, my sister, my love,*
> *   my dove, my perfect one;*
> *for my head is wet with dew,*
> *   my locks with the drops of the night.'*
> *(Song of Songs 5.2)*

Today some may find such devotion distasteful, but it points to the focus of our calling – union with God in joyful love – which was taken up by the German Benedictine, St Gertrude of Helfta (1256–1302). Gertrude received a series of visions similar to those later received by Margaret-Mary, leading her to write, among other works, *The Herald of Divine Love*: 'I want to enter the wounded heart of Jesus and immerse myself in this opened heart which is burning with love.' Gertrude was joined in this spirituality of 'nuptial mysticism' by other Sisters, together with the Beguine, St Mechthild of Magdeburg (c. 1207–c.82/94).

> *O Sacred Heart of Jesus, fountain of eternal life, Your Heart is a glowing furnace of Love. You are my refuge and my sanctuary. O my adorable and loving Saviour, consume my heart with the burning fire with which Yours is aflame. Pour down on my soul those graces which flow from Your love. Let my heart be united with Yours. Let my will be conformed to Yours in all things. May Your Will be the rule of all my desires and actions. Amen. (Prayer of St Gertrude)*

Three centuries later this nuptial devotion gradually affected the great Carmelite mystic John of the Cross, whose writings indicate the development of 'spiritual marriage' as revealed in his famous poem 'The Dark Night', which draws on the Song of Songs:

> *O night that was my guide!*
> *O darkness dearer than the morning's pride,*
> *O night that joined the lover*
> *To the beloved bride*
> *Transfiguring them each into the other.*

French School of Spirituality

While St John Eudes CIM (1601–80, a member of the so-called 'French School' which includes Cardinal de Bérulle, St Francis de Sales, etc.) honoured the Sacred Heart with an Office and established a feast it was de Sales who is considered of greater importance to the development of this devotion. Francis spoke of the union of the human and divine in Jesus as a 'nuptial kiss', writing of Jesus' Heart being 'a furnace of burning love which spreads its fiery flames in all directions, in heaven, on earth, and throughout the whole universe. ... Those divine fires transform all the hearts of heavenly lovers into so many furnaces of love for Him who is all love for them' (*Introduction to the Devout Life*, Introduction – Eighth Meditation). Francis, together with St Jane Frances de Chantal VHM (1572–1641), developed that particular spirituality known as 'Salesian' and founded the Order of the Visitation of Holy Mary (Visitation Order/Visitandines/VHM) which cherishes the virtues of gentleness and humility (Matthew 11.29). Francis' faith had been formed by the Jesuits and his spirituality reflects St Ignatius Loyola's (1491–1556) recognition of the power of the imaginative use of scripture whereby, using feelings and reasoning, were helped to connect with God's great

Seal of Visitation Order

goodness. Francis developed his own form of the Ignatian *Examen* as well as what is known as 'practical mysticism' concerning this union of the human and divine hearts which, in his book *The Sacred Heart of Jesus*, he described as the 'tender abode of divine love'.

ST MARGARET-MARY ALACOQUE VHM

Born in France, Margaret-Mary's childhood involved much suffering. When about 24 years old she had a vision of Christ being scourged and felt this to be a reproach to her 'worldly life' and sought admittance to the Visitation Order at Paray-le-Monial. Further apparitions occurred, each concerning the Sacred Heart and love of Jesus in the Eucharist.

Drawing by
St Margaret-Mary, 1685

On the Feast of St John the Evangelist (27 December 1673) Jesus, revealing his Heart, invited her to rest her head upon it thus taking the place of John at the Last Supper. She told of seeing a flaming throne which appeared transparent like crystal and more brilliant than the sun. The wound in Jesus' side appeared clearly, a crown of thorns surrounded his Heart which was surmounted by a cross and from which flames emerged. 'My Sacred Heart', Jesus told her, 'is so intense in its love for men and for you in particular that not being able to contain within it the flames of its burning charity, they must be transmitted through all means' (John Croiset SJ, *The Devotion to the Sacred Heart*, p. 44f.). She wrote: 'The kind Heart of Jesus opened for me like a large book, from which he made me read wonderful excerpts concerning his pure love.' He told her: 'I want you to read from this book of life which contains the science of love.'

Margaret-Mary recorded Jesus explaining that the instruments of his Passion signified the immense love he had for humankind, while the encircling crown of thorns represented humanity's 'sinfulness and ingratitude'. He reminded her of our need for a 'change of heart' which remains the focus of the devotion. She established a 'Holy Hour' – a time of adoration before the Blessed Sacrament – which can be kept alone or as part of a group and, on 16 June 1675, Jesus asked her to promote a feast in honour of his Heart while making various promises to those who venerated it and promoted the devotion. These included:

- consoling them when troubled;
- being their refuge in life and, especially, at death;
- blessing their undertakings;
- being an ocean of mercy;
- giving enthusiasm to those who are lukewarm.

Margaret-Mary explained that this devotion must involve regular confession and receiving Holy Communion, especially on nine consecutive monthly 'First Fridays' (recalling Good Friday). Many thought her deluded but when Bl. Claude de la Colombière SJ (1641–82) was appointed confessor to the Visitation sisters, he became convinced that her visions were genuine. He joined in her observances and wrote a book that, in time, helped spread devotion to both the Sacred Heart and that 'ocean of mercy' found in the Eucharist. He was subsequently sent to England to be chaplain to Queen Mary of Modena, second wife of King James II.

Margaret-Mary died on 17 October 1690 and on receiving the Last Rites said, 'I need nothing but God, and to lose myself in the Heart of Jesus.'

THE HEART OF MARY

Mary's Heart is that of the Mother whom Jesus commended to all Christians. Its importance is first seen in the way it was 'kissed' by the visitation of Love, which she pondered until it was conceived in her womb where, research confirms, the heart of mother and foetus beat as one. Because it was Mary's heart that helped form Jesus it is for love of the Son we honour the Mother; nor must we forget that the Trinity, the eternal communion of Love, *chose* her whose heart – thus her whole being – was closest to that of Jesus. It grew, was 'magnified', and must have been pure enough – Immaculate – to bear the Word for the world. On two separate occasions St Luke records that Mary 'treasured' moments of revelation concerning her Son in her heart (2.19 and 51) and, although some find her problematic, Mary's role in Christianity is crucial and so we need a proper devotion to her.

Into the solitariness of our heart Love's compassionate Word speaks and this Love, which made angels sing, shepherds kneel and Magi search, Mary saw enfleshed on straw in Bethlehem. Before that, when visiting her cousin Elizabeth, her soul was magnified, overflowing with joy and wonder, causing her heart to be a place of compassion and refuge (St Simeon prophesied that it would be pierced by a sword). But hearts corrupted by envy, greed, pride and selfishness can be blind to that wonder, generosity and humility which makes us fully human.

Among all the icons of Mary one, known as *The Softener of Evil Hearts*, depicts its piercing (hence is also known as

The Prophesy of Simeon) by seven arrows symbolizing particular occasions of sorrow. It's an expression of that tradition which sees her sufferings as a means to 'soften' hearts, not least when faced with Jesus' command to 'love' our enemies. By nature our heart will want to exclude them,  but the Sacred Heart loves even Christ's foes, seeing that, no matter how hard, it is by love alone that we can be reconciled. In praying for our enemies before this icon we must confess that we're also sinners and not accuse them of evil, but ask for help. Considered the 'Mother of Sorrows' Mary provides a way for anger to be 'softened' and give way to compassion.

Although few know of this devotion the oldest recorded prayer to Mary (*Sub tuum praesidium*, third–fourth century) is focused on this virtue:

> *We fly to your patronage, O holy Mother of God;*
> *despise not our petitions in our necessities,*
> *but deliver us always from all dangers,*
> *O ever glorious and blessed Virgin!*

More recently Pope Francis composed a beautiful prayer to Mary, the 'un-doer of knots'. In it he asks her to intercede with her Son to 'untie the knots that prevent us from being united with God, so that we, free from sin and error, may find Him in all things, may have our hearts placed in Him, and may serve Him always in our brothers and sisters'.

> *Merciful God,*
> *as we are embraced by your Divine Compassion*
> *found in the Hearts of Jesus and Mary,*
> *so may we live with that same compassion*
> *for all people and the whole of your creation.*

This we ask in the name of him whose Love enfolds all,
Jesus Christ our Lord.
Amen.

THE REFORMATION

At his cross we enter the heart of the universe ... All
the desire wherewith he longs after a returning sinner,
makes Him esteem a broken heart ... His heart is always
abroad in the midst of the earth, seeing and rejoicing in
His wonders there ... In all thy keeping, keep thy heart,
for out of it comes the issues of life and death. (Thomas
Traherne, c.1636–74, Anglican priest, theologian and
poet, Centuries of Meditations*)*

The rich veins of personal devotion which had existed for
more than a thousand years were severed by the Reformation and consequent 'Age of Reason' when a head/heart split,
together with a distaste for displays of emotion, developed.
No longer part of the universal (Roman) church the danger
of religion being controlled and determined by the nation-
state was real and the importance of the monastic life, with
its focus on purifying the heart, was gradually supplanted
by an emphasis on intellectual training. The use of images,
shrines, etc. was repudiated and popular devotions associated
with Jesus' humanity disappeared. The fact that, initially,
the Church in England became subservient to the monarch
helped energize the centrality of the nation-state while the
heresy of Arianism (Jesus wasn't truly divine) tempted many.

The consequent eighteenth-century Evangelical Revival
re-emphasized that God touches us through the heart and

enabled many to again recognize their sufferings mirrored in Jesus' Passion and death. John Wesley's heart was 'warmed' by Christ while his brother, Charles, wrote the famous hymn 'O for a heart to praise my God':

> *A heart from sin set free ...*
> *... a heart in every thought renewed,*
> *and full of love divine;*
> *perfect and right and pure and good –*
> *a copy, Lord, of thine.*

But feelings-inspired devotion was reputedly dismissed by one bishop who said: 'enthusiasm is a very wicked thing ... a very wicked thing indeed.' However, the subsequent Oxford (Anglo-Catholic) Movement rediscovered the Sacred Heart and Fr Andrew SDC (1869–1946), co-founder of the *Society of Divine Compassion*, expressed his love for it in various meditations including this popular hymn:

> *O dearest Lord, thy Sacred Heart*
> *with spear was pierced for me;*
> *O pour thy Spirit in my heart*
> *that I may live for thee.*

But such devotion wasn't simply intended to give a spiritual 'boost', or even make us feel better, but to assist our personal conversion – our *metanoia*. That's brought out in another of the apparitions to Margaret-Mary when Jesus said to her: 'Behold this Heart which has so loved human beings that it has spared nothing, even to exhausting and consuming itself, in order to give them proof of its love.'

> *Heart of Jesus, be my peace*
> *Thy wounded side my home*
> *Thy broken feet my following*

Thy pierced hands my guiding
Thy crown of thorns my exceeding rich reward
Thy cross my daily toil.
Thou knowest all, O my God
Thou knowest my wretchedness
Thou knowest that I love thee.
(Fr Gilbert Shaw, 1886–1967,
A Pilgrim's Book of Prayers, *p. 26)*

Reflections

- In what ways might devotion to the Passion of Christ touch people's hearts? Why might some avoid this, and what affect might that have on the way suffering is faced?
- Look again at the quotations offered in this chapter. Did any speak to you and why?
- Read Luke 1.39–47. What caused the baby in Elizabeth's womb to 'leap'?

A Salesian spiritual exercise

- **Place** yourself in God's presence.
- **Read** through a gospel scene concerning Jesus (e.g. the Visitation).
- **Ask** Jesus for assistance.
- **Compose** the scene.
- **Consider** images from it that touch you.
- **Resolve** 'convert feelings into understanding and then resolutions' (acts of the will).
- **Give thanks** for what you've experienced.

- **Offer** God the results of the meditation (Oblation) and ask that you might apply these fruits to your daily life.

Finally, Francis recommends choosing a 'spiritual nosegay', insights that have awoken your heart, to take with you and 'smell' throughout the day, just as people in his time took such nosegays to overcome the stench in the streets.

3

The Heart in Pilgrimage

... what can be seen is temporary,
but what cannot be seen is eternal.
(2 Corinthians 4.18)

The mind may have mountains, as Gerard Manley Hopkins
SJ wrote in his poem of that title, but the heart has chasms
few explore. We may be able to reach into vast inter-galactic
spaces, but many oceans are still to be plumbed, and the notion
of life as a 'pilgrimage', which is at the heart of Christianity, is
often forgotten. This is not helped if religion is seen to provide
simple solutions to complex life-issues or people are offered
tempting superficialities. What can be overlooked is that, as in
any loving relationship, God invites us to persevere in exploring the depths, an invitation made so that we can realize the
wonder of our being and that which needs our attention.

As we journey with God and begin to notice pleasant movements – feelings – within our heart we need to understand
that they don't occur simply to make us feel good; they're
invitations to respond with greater faith, hope and love. The
psalms point to the way certain human experiences such as
beauty, delight and desire nurture and expand the heart while
pointing to Sion/Jerusalem/Temple as their source and goal.
The longing and sense of emptiness we can sometimes experience without such feelings can drive us to divert attention to
the accumulation of 'stuff' – of wealth, power or even human
relationships. Yet the psalmist knows that, in the end, such

longings can only be fulfilled through our relationship with that Mystery we call God, for there will always be a 'beyond' calling to us. About this Augustine famously declared: 'Late have I loved you, beauty so old and so new: late have I loved you. And see, you were within and I was in the external world and sought you there, and in my unlovely state I plunged into those lovely created things which you made. You were with me, and I was not with you' (*Confessions*, 10).

Such awakening brings that spiritual consolation described by Ignatius Loyola as 'every increase in hope, faith and charity, and all interior joy which calls and attracts to heavenly things ... When this interior movement in the soul is caused [then] the soul comes to be inflamed with love of its Creator and Lord' (*Spiritual Exercises*, 316). When that occurs the memory of it, together with the insight it brings, will remain as a guide helping us discern the choices we must make. We know that God's call in Mary's Heart led to her 'yes' which reverberated down the centuries, but between call and response came fear, perplexity, pondering and questioning as her (Immaculate) Heart gradually opened to the Word and she could, with faith and love, freely say: 'Let it be with me according to your word.' That is the prayer we can make with confidence, whatever our particular vocation, as with St Paul we realize our primary calling: 'it is no longer I who live, but it is Christ who lives in me. And the life I now live in the flesh I live by faith in the Son of God, who loved me and gave himself for me' (Galatians 2.20).

However, if someone has never known love at any great depth they can feel overwhelmed if that emotion is suddenly experienced. Everyone's heart is also the object of darker, potentially corrosive movements which our forebears recognized as 'the passions' – gluttony, lust, avarice, anger, dejection, listlessness and pride – those unnatural (because not of God) desires which can cause confusion and, in time, do great damage. This was understood by the Desert Elders who sought places of solitude and silence in order to confront them, for they prevented attaining to that 'purity' of heart we'll consider in the next chapter. But if religion only offers safety, assurance and pleasure it is in danger of becoming escapism and of little use in dealing with our deepest needs.

> *Passion is an impulse of the soul contrary to nature.*
> *(St Maximus the Confessor, d.662,*
> Centuries on Love, 2, 16)

Discerning the Heart's call

Throughout the scriptures there are references to the under-lying way God's Heart lovingly yearns for us. From the time of our primal parents when God called to Adam, 'Where are you?', whether we realize it or not we are 'lost' unless we're in relationship with God. The theme that humankind and God are meant to exist in loving union is the witness of the Song of Songs together with the prophets and psalmists. Another great Anglican priest-poet, George Herbert (1593–1633), wrote of 'The Heart in Pilgrimage' in his poem 'Prayer (I)'. Others have noted that the heart has it's seasons because, just as the year unfolds, faith concerns that pilgrimage as we respond to the Spirit's invitation to journey into the presence of the Mystery in and yet beyond all things.

This is also the time to realize that, as Psalm 105 declares, to find God is to seek him constantly. Might *that* dynamic be built into our very being, our DNA ... a basic ingredient in the 'life-blood' of our humanity?

> *With my whole heart I seek you;*
> *do not let me stray from your commandments.*
> *I treasure your word in my heart,*
> *so that I may not sin against you.*
> *(Psalm 119.10–11)*

This is true of every particular church vocation – Religious Life, diaconate, priesthood, etc. – which are meant to focus our ongoing response to the call of Jesus' Heart. The good we set ours upon will continue to fashion us as we practise self-forgetfulness and attend to the Other who reaches out to the real 'me' beneath my masks. This involves deepening our relationship with the Lord, something reflected in the Second Week of Ignatius's *Exercises* when the retreatant considers Jesus' invitations together with his gospel until they can say: 'I desire and choose poverty with Christ poor rather than wealth; contempt with Christ laden with it rather than honours. Even further, I desire to be regarded as a useless fool for Christ, who before me was regarded as such, rather than as a wise or prudent person in this world' (*Exercises*, 167). However, no matter how hard we try to discern the right choice in life, the final decision will always involve those acts of faith, hope and love which God will accept and work with.

But beware that monstrous voice of perfectionism which can deafen us to the fact that our 'imperfections' also leave us vulnerable to God. Ignatius points to the paradox that what the church needs is more 'fools for Christ', saints who are so madly in love with Jesus that they will do extraordinary things for him. People like the reluctant Second World War RAF hero and son of an Anglican priest, John Bradburne OFS (1921–79), who, after military service, became a Roman Catholic and 'vagabond for God' (also calling himself God's jester) until finally settling at a leprosy centre in Zimbabwe. from which he was abducted and killed in 1979 during the Rhodesian War of Independence. This latter-day Francis of Assisi became an advocate for those who lived there, sharing fully in their life and, as a member of Francis' Third Order, sang the full Daily Office and is now on the path to beatification.

'God's love within you is your native land.
So search none other, never more depart.
For you are homeless save God keeps your heart.'
(Servant of God John Bradburne OFS)

CALLED TO THE RELIGIOUS LIFE

We must go forth into the world with a heart which
imitates the Heart of Jesus. It is for us to have that Heart
really communicated to us; it is for us to ask him to take
our hearts away and give us His – that Heart which he
yearns to find reproduced. (Retreat for the All Saints
Sisters of the Poor, 1868, Look to the Glory, *p. 30)*

Listening to Jesus' call some will sense the call to give themselves wholeheartedly to him through the Religious Life
– monastic or apostolic – which is a particular expression of
the way all Christians are called to live by way of those vows
affirmed at Baptism. Its existence is an important gift to the
church's witness to the primacy of the First Commandment
and she needs to value, learn from and nurture this calling.

In the Anglican Communion Religious Life re-emerged, in
part, as a response to the appalling nineteenth-century social
conditions in cities (and countryside) where many saw the
corrupting danger of setting your heart on the accumulation
of wealth and possessions. Some founder/resses turned, in
particular, to Jesus' Sacred Heart as a means of overcoming
this tendency: the initial (1894) *Rule* of the Society of Divine
Compassion (SDC), founded in the poverty of London's East
End, declared that it was 'dedicated in love and veneration to
the Sacred Heart of Jesus, Our Lady, and Saint Francis'.

The First World War led to the development of various initiatives aimed at redirecting the heart of ordinary Christians to love the poor, one of which was the (Anglican) *Confraternity of Divine Love*. Founded by Elizabeth Ann Hodges and some friends, their prayer was, 'Baptize us, O God, with the Holy Spirit and kindle in us the fire of Thy Love', and the symbol of the Confraternity was the Cross, at the centre of which was a heart enfolding the word 'JESUS'. As it developed it quickly gave birth in to the (Franciscan-inspired) *Order of St Elizabeth of Hungary* (OSEH) to work especially among women and orphans in London, Sussex and Australia while also pioneering Retreats. Later (Mother) Elizabeth OSEH wrote: 'The realization that the Sacred Heart has been placed by the Incarnation in the very centre of our being is our inspiration and our strength' (*Into the Deep*, p. 43).

Religious Orders such as this remind the church that it mustn't allow its life to be overwhelmed by 'Martha'. Although they returned late to the Church of England monastic/contemplative Orders are special, tangible witnesses to the primacy of 'Mary's' vocation to quiet listening. The Life was valued until the Reformation, but the subsequent Age of Reason/Enlightenment gave greater attention to the head/intellect, giving rise to René Descartes' (1596–1650) famous dictum, 'I think therefore I am.' Many have questioned that, and Metropolitan Kallistos Ware (1934–2022), in a 2005 lecture at the Institute for Orthodox Christian Studies in Cambridge, suggested that a better definition of what it means to be a person would be, 'I love, therefore I am', once more placing the heart at the centre of our being.

It is love which motivates (our sisters)
to follow the way of the evangelical councils;
it is love which binds them to God, and to each other;
it is the spirit of humility and gentleness.
(Rule of the Visitation Order)

CALLED TO ORDINATION

Everyone who is baptized is a member of Christ's Body and so has a share in his Heart. This is where those called into sacramental ministry, especially priesthood, need to have their own heart set, for it is love (of God first) which is their call and means of sanctification. If it isn't then their vocation will risk being undermined.

Pope Benedict XVI observed: '[The priest's] mission is to be a mediator, a bridge that connects, and thereby to bring human beings to God, to His redemption, to His true light, to His true life' (Rome, 18 February 2010), which requires them to have one foot planted in the world and the other in Christ. A decade later Pope Francis underlined this in his Apostolic Exhortation, *Querida Amazonia*, when he said that 'the sacrament of Holy Orders ... configures him to Christ the priest' (87), and to be 'configured' involves having the heart fashioned by Christ's. This needs to have begun before ordination training, which is often so concerned with theological formation that adequate attention to the ongoing need to nurture a relationship with God can be lacking. The spirituality of the Divine Office and Eucharist along with a recognition of the place of meditation and silence need to be understood lest ordinands fail to understand the vital need to focus on their relationship with Jesus.

This is a fundamental and costly aspect of every Christian's development. It's easy (and dangerous) for 'church' or ministry to become one's primary focus rather than the desire to grow in the love of Jesus, of what he loves and how he calls us to live. Devotion to the Sacred Heart helps refocus our heart into this primary calling of which ministry is an expression. Ideas, passions, projects or causes, no matter how worthy, need to be informed by that Heart which moulds who we become – in *his* Will is our peace.

It's easy for a minister's life with Christ to be subsumed by their 'work' which then becomes the focus of their prayer. This can be particularly true for those working in places such as prisons where profoundly dark, life-denying forces operate and chaplains etc. need to develop that silent prayer which opens them to the Heart of Light. Giving time to this may be hard but it's of immense importance, for from that Heart flow those streams that can prevent the darkness becoming overwhelming (John 7.38). Recourse to the Sacrament of Reconciliation will also provide an important means of refocusing the heart into its primary vocation, for the quality of our love will be determined by the heart's purity.

A bruised heart

Many clergy will find that anger – even vitriol – is directed at them. Not only does their role make them targets, but their vocation also attracts certain 'dark' spiritual/psychic forces seeking to extinguish the light they carry. Sharing in Christ's priesthood involves clergy in his costly, redemptive love for the world. which can also, at times, lead to sleepless-ness, despair or even depression. It's important to take care of ourselves, but equally important is to 'know ourselves'; to understand enough of ourselves so that as little transference occurs as possible with, for example, a parishioner. Clergy need to recognize that it may not be them but their role that is the primary cause of someone's reactions.

It's also easy to hold on to any sense of external disturb-ance, to try and 'sort things out' or 'understand it' to the point it begins to stick like Velcro. In such circumstances there's a need not only to pray for illumination, but to also find ways of detaching ourselves from the disturbance by redirecting our attention of the Heart of Christ. Priests can place the disturbance on the paten with the Host when sharing in Christ's sacrificial, eucharistic oblation for he would transform whatever we enfold in his offering to the Father by the power of the Spirit.

For all these reasons a minister's life in Christ needs to be central because, when neglected, s/he will become ever more vulnerable to those darker, hidden forces.

Priesthood and sanctity

The Daily Office and – when possible – Eucharist, prayerful times before the Blessed Sacrament, Quiet Days, annual Retreats and adequate rest are not optional extras in busy lives, but essential ingredients for vocational living. In the late nineteenth century Fr George Congreave SSJE preached a sermon that still seems remarkably relevant:

> *It is by the multitude and activity of its organizations that the church begins to be popularly recognized as passing from the condition of religious deadness to religious vitality … But there is no time or place for anything but activity and bustle. We must always begin something new … One result of this is spiritual weariness … I have little time left, and less inclination, to pray … the interior life I must leave to others … Saint Paul gives us a very different note of the Catholic Church in its best state – the note of sanctity: 'this is the will of God even your sanctification … Sanctification, sanctity, holiness: these notions can seem to belong to another world.*

So it is that people (rightly) hope that the lives of clergy will exhibit *something* of what they expect to find in Christ. This isn't to say that they must be particularly pious – incorporation into the incarnate Christ means having a true 'earthiness' (humility, not crudeness). It's for such reasons they need to be careful, for example, of their speech, actions and appearance, remembering that 'he must increase, but I must decrease' (John 3.30).

Over the years I've come to realize the truth of that saying 'Heart speaks to heart', words chosen by St John Henry Newman (the great nineteenth-century former Anglican) as his motto. His French contemporary, St John Mary Vianney, was more specific, describing the priesthood as the 'love of the Heart of Jesus' for if that doesn't animate a calling, what does? Someone might be an eloquent preacher, brilliant theologian, fine liturgist, exciting missioner or relevant social commentator, but if the heart isn't seeking union with the love of the Sacred Heart, what might form it and what will it offer?

Lost hearts

Like any in the caring profession clergy must also consider to what extent a need-to-be-needed, approved of or liked drives their ministry. Absence of these in early life can cause vulnerability to the ceaseless demands that are never satisfied unless their causes are addressed. Others can experience a sense of emptiness or fear being unlovable, leaving them vulnerable to an urge to find love, and because love can have a sexual element the two can become confused. So it's important to understand our inner 'drivers' – a matter for the ministry of spiritual direction.

> *Upon my bed at night*
> *I sought him whom my soul loves;*
> *I sought him, but found him not ...*
> *(Song of Songs 3.1)*

The matter of having an 'empty' heart can lead priests (and others) to mask it with busyness to such an extent that they're disinclined to pray – or even rest – because that would expose them to what they fear. The place of 'Ordinary Time' is dismissed as everything must produce results (not helped if under pressure to perform), do better and succeed. At such times they can criticize others in order to deflect attention from their own emptiness, sense of failure, inadequacy or pride, thus 'boosting' themselves. This can happen whether one lives alone or is partnered – although the presence of another or close friends can help. It might also drive them to become subject to certain addictive behaviours and the adrenaline rush that follows which can, once over, leave feelings of irritability, guilt or fear of stillness and solitude. Thus the place of aloneness with God gets sidelined together with that prayer of faithful, loving waiting which needs to be part of a minister's Rule of Life – attention to these nurtures our foundations.

Heart of priestly calling

Clergy, then, need to keep their heart's eye orientated to the Sacred Heart lest they become lost in the multitude of hearts they encounter. There'll always be times when we feel we're in a dry, lifeless wilderness, or become exhausted by pastoral care and lack support. Those are reasons why it's essential that the heart is directed to God and not the church and that primary attention is given to drinking from the waters of life springing from Christ's Heart (John 4.1f.).

For their vocation to flourish (which doesn't mean successful) clergy need to be rooted in God's love and live for God's glory – which is the purpose of all life. Primarily that will be expressed through worship, which is our ultimate vocation only fully realized when, through Love's purging, we're led to the purity of Divine union. Yet we can begin to give expression to that as we realize our part in the great chorus of praise singing with the Creator. It's in the loving exchange of gifts – the gift of self and the gift of God – that vocation is realized and flourishes: we need to shift from self-centredness to Christ-centredness; to keep ever fresh a deepening desire for God's gift – Jesus.

External role – inner dwelling

This call of holiness is central to any Christian vocation. We need confidence in our vocation rather than the arena of our, or others', expectations or projections. Clergy need to draw from those deep wells of prayer and scriptural meditation as antidotes to overwork so that their role – minister, vicar, rector, chaplain, etc. – doesn't dominate. A proficient spiritual director can help us process our inner life and make sure we're aware of what's drawing us – and what's *driving* us. Whatever we're called to do needs to express who we're called to become: the Holy Spirit is co-creating with us as we seek to listen and respond in our desire to live to God's glory.

Pope St Gregory (c.540–604), who developed that plainsong which, drawing on ancient sacred chant, uniquely speaks from Heart to heart to arouse its yearning, has been called the 'Doctor of Desire'. He believed all Christian life needs to be built on longing for God, something anyone concerned with Christian formation needs to consider. The hidden power of desire is illustrated by the way advertisers offer something attractive (and cheap) but only superficially satisfying – no wonder people can be disinclined to consider anything that might come at greater cost. Gregory also warned clergy about the danger of allowing themselves to be overwhelmed by the world's cares and concerns, telling them to practise contemplative living because it provides a balance to the world's demands.

Heart and church – lost in your call

It's easy to let externals determine how we develop and if clergy let their vocation be determined by their relationship with the church any initial Divine desires will become submerged to the extent that contact with their inner-self and the heart of who they are – their 'soul' – will become lost. If someone finds it difficult to express their relationship with God apart from what they do, then it's important for them to re-member their primary calling. This can easily become overwhelmed by the responsibilities that go with ordination – being a bishop or their representative, an office-holder or filler-in-of-posts on the PCC, a person of some social standing, an example of what people perceive as an institution, an occupier of a rung on a ladder to be climbed. Has the person God called as a minister of grace and witness to the Kingdom become addicted to their *role*? Are they still guardians of the Divine Mysteries and proclaimers of the Kingdom, or have they become officers of the Church of England PLC identified by a business-like logo ⊕ ...

But it's never too late to take a step back and consider afresh how one relates with the Master. What the church is called to offer and encourage is a spirituality speaking into our deeper needs and desires rather than being, apparently, externally attractive. Some will need to move from relating to a 'sky-daddy', problem-solver or divine demagogue to realizing their fundamental need – to live at one with our mysterious God, creation and ourselves. This will be aided by 'interiority', the nurturing of a counter-cultural, contemplative approach to life, illustrated by the story of Jesus' visit to Martha and Mary (Mark 10.38f.).

We are come to God not by navigation but by love.
(Ascribed to Augustine of Hippo)

Career or calling?

Yet it seems that success and productivity rule even in parts of the church. What were once known as 'vocational' pathways – healthcare, education, social work, etc. – are now often referred to as 'industries' and even clergy can refer to their 'job'. Is it any wonder that we're often judged by what we do rather than who we're called to become?

If 'church' claims our primary attention it can cause us to be driven by the energy of self-will masquerading as faith, or we can believe our 'flourishing' will only be possible if certain ways are opened up, leading to priesthood being considered a career – vicar, dean, bishop ... Pope? Ministry might thrive and people be inspired by us, which can be very exciting, but without humility – that virtue linked to the need for fortitude – the bright light of our abilities can cast dark shadows; we can become envious of others and any failures and short-comings we have can distress rather than humble us.

Once our calling turns into a job and we feel judged by success or failure then when ministry ends we can be left with the question, 'How can I be a minister/priest when I can't do ministerial/priestly things?' That touches on the matter of our 'being beneath the role': have I any purpose apart from what I do? Does priesthood have meaning apart from ministry? How can I develop and maintain healthy and satisfying relationships? Others may find that what has come to be regarded as essential to making life worthwhile – the ability to freely enjoy social interactions, holidays in the sun, team sports, parties and so on – are denied them and the question then arises: 'What's it all about?' Life, that is.

I know that's *the* existential question, but it's a real question. At some point we can begin to wonder if our lives have any purpose, especially when full-time working draws to a close or our partner dies (or isn't found). Clergy can also, like others, suffer from burn-out and while rest is necessary so too is a retreat in the Heart of God (and time with a Religious Order offers the opportunity to be with a community centred into the healing Heart of God). Such bleak times offer opportunities to rediscover our relationship with him whose Heart would enfold us.

One final thought. If those engaged in dynamic ministry find themselves humbled by circumstances, sacred or secular, they need to remember that as their persona might crumble the child of God is still held in Jesus' Heart. Confession and absolution may be necessary, but then there will be nothing separating them from that Heart nor preventing the call to holiness as St Paul's profound insight tells us:

> *Let the same mind be in you that was in Christ Jesus,*
> *who, though he was in the form of God,*
> *did not regard equality with God*
> *as something to be exploited,*
> *but emptied himself,*
> *taking the form*
> *of a slave ...*
> *(Philippians 2.5–7)*

Reflections

- How do you perceive your vocation apart from the role you fulfil?
- What first drew you to that expression of the love of the Heart of Jesus? What is there about him you now want to express? Is there a word in your heart to which you desire to give expression? ... Dig deeper ... recall what led, moved, urged you to give *this* expression to God's continuing call that is still heard – maybe dimly – in your heart.

A prayer

Most High, glorious God,
enlighten the darkness of my heart.
Give me right faith, sure hope and perfect charity.
Fill me with understanding and knowledge
that I may fulfil your command.
(Francis of Assisi, Prayer Before the Crucifix*)*

A suggestion

Arrange for a representation of the Sacred Heart to be placed on a board inside your church. Provide pens and 'post-it' notes and invite people to place around it their prayers and reflections.

A short liturgy

HEART SPEAKS TO HEART (SH.2) *can be found in* Appendix 2 *and could be added to an Office. It can also be found online:* https://johnfrancisfriendship.co.uk/sacred-hearts

4

Abiding in the Heart

'The good person out of the good treasure
of the heart produces good,
and the evil person out of evil treasure produces evil;
for it is out of the abundance of the heart
that the mouth speaks.'
(Luke 6.45)

Although the Gospels rarely mention Jesus' Heart (which he described as 'humble' in Matthew 11.29) St John does record a deeply intimate and prolonged invitation to 'abide' in him. It's contained within his great 'I am' statement about being the Vine and his disciples the branches (John 15, esp. v.9) offered in the context of the Last Supper and so making clear the eucharistic overtones of this close, personal 'indwelling'.

Such indwelling began when the Word entered the womb of Mary who's heart helped form his. The message of the Sacred Heart involves a recognition that life involves commitment and commitment is particularly challenging to those wanting instant gratification. Our heart can easily be attracted elsewhere and, as a consequence, will sometimes experience desolation – caused by a lack of faith, hope and love. Apparitions of the Sacred Heart were received by those living the monastic life, which involves a vow of Stability as they 'abide' with Christ through thick and thin, but there are many ways we can 'abide'. While John's Gospel contains no birth narrative it does, from early on (1.38), detail times when Jesus invites people to 'stay' with him, which may have concerned getting to know him until, finally, supporting him during his Passion. All this 'abiding', as uncomfortable as it can be, is necessary for any deeper revelation.

As a child I lived – 'abided' – with my parents and although I could never know them as well as they knew each other this began that same development Jesus must have experienced through his 'hidden years' with Mary and Joseph. That is a reminder of the importance of times in our relationship with God when, at a superficial level, nothing appears to happen yet, like seed sown in good soil, the heart is learning important lessons. Much later I rented a room in someone's flat and came to know them a little better as they slowly opened aspects of themselves to me. Then, as a Franciscan, I lived with other Brothers, each having our own cell/room and developed a deeper friendship with some. Eventually, after meeting my partner, we agreed to share our lives and a home, and it's into a similar intimacy Jesus invites us so that, as he abides in our humanity, we might share in his divinity. What kind of intimacy with Jesus do you seek?

This invitation to abide as branches of the Vine, given as he faced his Passion, concerns sharing life with him and what greater privilege can we have than to abide in his Heart where love is nurtured? Where we can be, like John, his 'bosom friend'? Realizing the utter wonder of this invitation we need to let Jesus' words sink into our heart: 'As the Father has loved me, so I have loved you; *abide in my love*' (John 15.9). How often do we reflect on that invitation? To make a home in his Heart and be at one with him in love? This doesn't override the love for our partner, if we have one; it is the Love behind all loves, a call to dwell, be at home with, share in his way of living. It's where we can stay if we love him and abandon ourselves to his will, for 'you have died, and your life is hidden with Christ in God' (Colossians 3.3).

Seeing with the heart

John's Gospel is one of particular intimacy leading to Jesus' extended prayer to the Father in the power of the Spirit during the Last Supper. This was when Jesus opened his Heart to the twelve disciples expressing awareness of that divine 'glory' he shared with them and wants everyone to 'see' as, at the climax, he prays for complete oneness. Such 'seeing' and 'knowing' is with the heart's eye; we're invited into the depth of this revelation concerning that glory spoken of 'in the beginning' and revealed on the cross. Yet, paradoxically, it is there that Jesus' awareness of this very union with the Father will seem to vanish, causing his heart-rending cry, 'My God, my God, why have you forsaken me?' (Matthew 27.46).

But if religious faith is sidelined then the ageless and cosmic importance of Jesus' Passion and death ceases to be realized. Why bother with something that will involve the place of suffering on life's journey – especially as the 'world' offers many easily obtained distractions? An over-emphasis on the 'here and now', the immanent and material, the pleasurable and easily rewarding can result in the mystery of divine darkness being regarded as foolish, the preserve of the self-selected 'religious' rather than being of universal value. And the consequence? We lose touch with something foundational to our humanity.

> *Just as he who looks at the sun cannot but fill his eyes with light so he who always gazes intently into his heart cannot fail to be illumined. (Hesychios the Priest, d. 450, On Watchfulness and Holiness, para. 108, The Philokalia)*

The marginalizing of faith and, counter-intuitively, growing influence of religious fundamentalism raises the question of how far the church might have overlooked the importance of the interior life? People might talk of 'going to church' or 'winning disciples', but they're aspects of the outward expression of our faith – which involves that long path of transformation celebrated through the Eucharist. In the busy-ness and noisiness of life (even of churches) we must remember that our primary call is to heed Jesus' invitation to this at-oneness. And that doesn't simply apply to individuals – as Mother Earth suffers from our carelessness, greed and lust (which we're in danger of exporting to the stars) we mustn't ignore the way she has a heart needing care, which will be the subject of the final chapter.

THE HEART AND PRAYER

Prayer continues in the desire of the heart,
though the understanding be employed on outward things.
(John Wesley, A Plain Account of Christian Perfection,
Ch. 11)

Our 'spiritual' life with Christ benefits from heeding the – normally silent – movements of the Spirit of the Beloved. Prayer is the means whereby Lover and beloved communicate, that movement that leaves us, and all creation, vulnerable to the love of God. It's an offering of love to the One who is Love and requires deep listening and a discerning ear. This was the approach of that old farmer who, sitting in his church before the tabernacle containing the Blessed Sacrament, explained to St John-Marie Vianney (1786–1859): 'I look at him and He looks at me' – and, we might add, 'we tell each other we love each other.' This happens as prayer moves from mind to heart, from ego to soul, from an act of will to a response to the Spirit.

Brother Lawrence of the Resurrection OCD (c.1614–91) wrote, 'It is not necessary for being with GOD to be always at church; we may make an oratory of our heart, wherein to retire from time to time, to converse with Him in meekness, humility, and love' (*The Practice of the Presence of God*, Seventh Letter). This approach concerns meditation (or contemplation) on God's presence, which isn't intended to make us 'feel' better but to nurture the heart. To offer an empty space in which the Holy Spirit can work, drawing us ever more deeply into God's Heart.

However, at some point there's likely to come a time when what might have begun as a wondrous experience will lose its attraction, when God seems absent. It's then we need to move to loving God for God's sake and not for any 'felt experience' we may have. We have to learn to walk by faith, believing in the love of God even when it might not be felt. This will be a time of patient waiting when it's easy to feel nothing's happening, or we wonder if we've taken a wrong turn – or simply become bored. Of this experience Paul explains that 'having nothing I possess all things' (2 Corinthians 6.10).

Silence and the heart

Yet during this waiting the mind is usually active. Just like the movement of the stars that process cannot be prevented – what matters is that the heart is set on God, for now is the time when the two can be present to each other. Such a loving desire will help us discover that prayer concerns more than asking God for things – meditation and contemplation enable us to descend into the heart where the Spirit, the breath of God, affects her work as the simple act of breathing acts as a bridge from head to heart. For, as someone once said, the heart is the organ of contemplation.

Some worry this will make them 'open to the devil' and while we need to reflect on what emerges during prayer remember that Christ is more powerful than Satan, and don't ignore two thousand years of wisdom concerning the contemplative way. At a time when secular (and much Christian) culture has lost awareness of the contemplative life it needs to be taught, encouraged and practised in the churches, otherwise those who find they need to give attention to the heart can feel they're encountering a strange wilderness into which they shouldn't trespass. Gatherings for silent prayer are particularly important because they connect us with the heart of each person in a hidden but powerful way.

> *A genuine mystery is protected by silence that remains after analysis and explanation. We approach the mystery of our being by respectful listening, by recollecting our experience, by cherishing paradox and, above all, by loving what we cannot reduce to understanding. (Sam Keen,* Fire in the Belly, *p. 219)*

Silence in prayer and worship offers a means whereby the heart can be cleansed of its dross and hardness and enables openness to God – a heart that is never silent or still can easily become lost in the cacophony of life.

Aging and loss

As nature's seasons change to enable life's cycle so do we. We begin to have intimations of mortality, and may sense an absence of those feelings that once indicated God's presence – sometimes suddenly but usually gradually, imperceptibly, the things we once held important lose their attraction. In maturing we need to let go of aspects of the past in order that more subtle, quieter movements can occur. The heart may still relish the things that gave life but, slowly, it needs to adjust to deeper, massive shifts occurring as we move into maturity, old age and, finally, death when we shall have the opportunity of being cleansed of sin by the wonder of Love's fire and come to dwell in God's presence. For how could the Heart of him who loves us not always desire to unite us with the light and love of God?

If our spirituality has been 'feelings' based the gradual diminishment of 'affective' prayer which can come with old age can be quite confusing and discomforting. Yet there's an invitation here to begin attending to those 'passions' addressed earlier which need to be overcome if we're to be more fully present to the Heart of God. Such a realization can be important as we experience more physical pain, our ability to focus attention slowly diminishes, we fall asleep at unexpected times (not least during prayer) and become forgetful. It is then that a well of desolation can open as we have less to fill our time, children leave home, our circle of friends diminishes, a life-partner dies and we may move into care, all of which can be heightened if we've struggled with a deep sense of loneliness and looked to externals (including religion) to fill our emptiness, leaving us, in T. S. Eliot's telling phrase, with that 'growing terror of nothing to think about' (Four Quartets, East Coker, III). How easy, then, to become 'hollow men' (and women), fearful or unaware of what lies in our inner world or grasping at the latest worship song, popular form of meditation practice – or simply abandoning God altogether.

Yet, paradoxically, St Isaac the Syrian (c.613–700) assures us (Treatise 65) that we should 'welcome' such confusing, silent times because they produces fruit 'about which the tongue cannot speak'. At first 'compelling' ourselves to still the passions we discover that we're drawn deeper into the heart where silence and stillness is to be nurtured so that our inner, warring voices – our passions – can be stilled.

Passion and prayer

Nowhere in the scriptures does Jesus say we'll feel his love or that our heart will be moved – nor, thankfully, does the 'existence' of God depend on those feelings (an aspect of a self-centred culture?). It's not the *feelings* associated with God we're to seek, which would be a form of idolatry, but God's-self – an encounter often occurring in darkness, but a darkness that draws us because within it is the One upon whose face we cannot gaze and live, as God explained to Moses (Exodus 33.20):

> *When you begin you find only darkness*
> *and a cloud of unknowing.*
> *Reconcile yourself to wait in the darkness*
> *as long as necessary after him who you love.*
> (Anon., The Cloud of Unknowing, *14th century, Ch. 3)*

This can be deeply confusing as it seems we're no longer pray-ing; but the Spirit, knowing what we desire, would draw us into a place of more perfect love where the passions are less controlling. We're being invited to embark on a movement that isn't dependent on pleasurable feelings, but on simply offering time (e.g. 15–30 minutes) for that silent prayer of longing love even though it's constantly interrupted by leap-ing, chattering monkeys as we seek to descend into the heart.

And if you want to quieten a raging heart and mind fired by anger, guilt, hurtful memories and so on, or look to faith to give you peace, what you probably need to do is to speak honestly with your priest or a spiritual director who, by the grace of the Holy Spirit, can help your slow healing.

Beneath all these movements God is unconsciously moving the heart to deeper love (and encouraging its purification), although all we might feel is a dim sense of being drawn. 'The contemplative', wrote Fr Gilbert Shaw, 'lifts the heart in dependence on God – that the love of God may descend to become its heart-beat' (*The Contemplative, the World, and the Church*, unpublished paper, 1959). At this point we might find an attraction to that profound Orthodox 'Prayer of the Heart', the Jesus Prayer, or even to simply repeating the Holy Name with the breathing: *'Je-sus'*. What matters is our faithfulness to prayer as, with patience, the Spirit engages in the life-long work of transformation. This is not only the prayer of the humble-hearted, those who admit the truth about themselves, but the test of faithfulness.

> *I offer thee the only thing I have,*
> *My capacity to be filled by Thee.*
> *(Anon., Sufi saying)*

Should you wonder whether you're on the right track one way to check is to notice if you have a growing sense of compassion for others and less concern for self. You may also experience material buried in your deep unconscious surfacing – some of which might cause you to react, worry or try to re-bury the material – but this is an important movement in the heart's calling to wholeness and holiness and another matter for spiritual direction.

Intercession, compartmentalized living and abiding in love

At this point it might seem that intercession and thanksgiving have no place in prayer. But both are expressions of love so, confronted with the struggle between good and evil, darkness and light, we need to stand with the suffering Christ as, in the power of the Spirit, he offers his Heart-felt prayer to the Father.

The problem is that we often locate 'prayer' in a particular time or place to the extent that, at other times, we find ourselves simply longing for 'space' to 'be with God'. But this can be an aspect of the way we tend to compartmentalize life – *this* is when we work, rest, play ... and intercede. Some live in their heads and like to 'think about things' – even God – but the wisdom of the ages was captured in that insight of St Simeon the New Theologian back in the eleventh century: 'place your mind in your heart ... keep it there ... and let it constantly abide there' *(Writings from the Philokalia*, p. 158). So it is that, at any time of day or night, whatever is happening, we can descend into our private 'oratory of the heart' and be present to God with all that's in our heart. There we need to pray for an increase in those graces of faith, hope and love as we desire that mind and heart, God and self, prayer and life be integrated until, as Paul said, we are to 'pray without ceasing' (1 Thessalonians 5.17).

Heart of Jesus, increase in me faith, hope and love.

It's not that we ought to ignore or dismiss the mind, but that it needs enfolding in the heart, our unifying centre, lest it dominate and detach us from the rest of our being. The problem is that, for some, belief has become academic – 'I can assent to this; I can't believe that' – but there's a story told of a priest in Africa who, seeking to translate St John's Gospel into the local dialect and not finding a word equating with 'believe', asked a local villager for help and, after listening, the villager simply explained: 'To believe means to listen with the heart.'

Ultimately it's love that must inform all prayer, all we do and who we are. Mary, the contemplative, belongs with Martha, the activist (Luke 10.38–42), for action indicates and nurtures the love in our hearts.

Mountains, cloud and fire – contemplation and meditation

But there are other ways we can 'know' connected with that sixth sense, intuition. 'Knowing another is endless', wrote Nan Shepherd in her book *The Living Mountain*, 'the thing to be known grows with the knowing' (p. 108). There will be times when, consciously or not, we sit quietly before a painting, sunset, sea or landscape and simply wonder. But contemplative *prayer*, in whatever form, is the call to be lovingly present to our hidden God (cf. Luke 24.13f.).

Orthodox and Western masters of the spiritual life agree that God is – must be – hidden from mortal gaze (Exodus 33.20). Throughout the scriptures, especially in John's Gospel, there's a recognition that it's with the eye of the heart we need to 'see', for it is through the heart we're to gaze on the Beloved. 'Lift up your heart to God with humble love,' writes the anonymous author of *The Cloud of Unknowing*, 'and mean God himself, and not what you get out of him' (Ch. 3). They then write of the need to use a single word to 'beat' on this cloud hiding 'the brightness of Love' (Ch. 7) with the 'sharp dart of longing love' (cf. Exodus 17.6 and 24.18). As a faithful lover reaches out to the heart of their beloved so God reaches out to ours and we're to nurture a similar heart, for prayer without love is life-less and can become self-centred. Love for the 'other' (especially a partner) is a lens, an icon, *through* which we gaze lest we become self-absorbed. Prayer must be moved by a desire to grow in this Godly love and a desire to live as Christ lived – to pray in and from his loving, Sacred Heart. Here is that place (hidden by that thick cloud) where treasure lies.

Sufi Islam, recognizing the importance of the heart, also developed teaching and practices concerning the 'remembrance of God' (*dhikr*) through repeatedly invoking God's 'Name' in order to imprint it on the heart. Like the mantric

Jesus Prayer it begins on the lips (Oral Prayer) with the aid of the mind (Mental Prayer) before descending into the heart. This offers a simple way to cultivate that interior silence that can calm the 'raging seas' in our heart where, by the grace of God and commitment of our will, the prayer takes residence and becomes united with the heart's beat. We 'in-breathe' the love of God (the Breath/Spirit of God) and breathe out our self-centredness, our breath being that 'golden thread' lovingly channelling inner and outer, making two hearts beat as one. So, rather than fearing our depths, we need to cultivate inner stillness in order that, as God wills, our darkness can be turned into light. As Fr Colin CSWG said at the Requiem for Fr Gregory CSWG:

> *The human person should become a still centre, always waiting on God and invoking his Holy Spirit, so as to embrace the whole world in his or her life of prayer and obedience to his will. In each of us it is the heart that has to be that still centre, the dwelling place of the Spirit, the place of offering, the wellspring of prayer and love for others.*

Personal growth

Some will look to religious bodies – churches etc. – to provide acceptance, compassion and love, yet although they're important that's not their primary purpose. They exist to enable individuals to grow in wholeness and holiness as they love one another and give themselves to worship and the teachings of the faith. Yet while a warm and caring community can be attractive, given human failings (sinfulness), it's likely they'll fail at some point, which is one reason why the church needs to help people grow in their inner life. The world has much to offer, but the church mustn't sideline its treasury of contemplative practices – its most important 'fresh expression'.

Many may prefer the light and laughter they find in some churches but, more importantly, they will need help in facing the darkness and warfare encountered in their heart which, ultimately, envelops God's presence. Rather than seeing Christianity as a prop it exists to lovingly enable Christ's presence, offer ways to overcome sin and evil and lead people to the vision of God.

CARMELITE SPIRITUALITY

For me, prayer is a surge of the heart;
it is a simple look turned toward heaven,
a cry of recognition and of love
in times of trial as well as in times of joy.
(St Thérèse of Lisieux OCD, 1873–97, Story of a Soul)

There will always be some who dismiss religion as an escape for people who can't face life, but those who have sought to respond to God's invitation into a deeper relationship know this requires being stripped of any unnecessary 'props' we've accumulated along the way. And that can take us along what is known as the *via negativa*, the way of darkness and loss, explored in both Eastern and Western spiritual traditions which Eliot alludes to in *East Coker* (*Four Quartets*) when he writes of travelling 'by a way wherein there is no ecstasy ...', an unknowing way that can, therefore, be deeply disconcerting.

Eliot, who admitted to being a deeply committed Ango-Catholic, was referring to what happens on the journey to the Heart of Christ by sharing Carmelite wisdom. Carmelites form a monastic Order that probably developed as a number of returning twelfth-century Crusaders settled on Mount

Carmel (north-west Israel) as hermits in imitation of St Elijah (1 Kings 19.9f.). Considering the heart their true 'cell' they recognize *conversatio morum*, conversion of life, as central to their calling.

Four centuries later one of their number, St Teresa of Jesus (of Avila), experienced her heart being pierced by the 'dart of love' (transverberation). Her writings include the image of an 'interior castle' into which the soul is invited to journey, a castle with seven 'mansions' where it is

> ... *not so essential to think much as to love much ... Love does not consist in great sweetness of devotion, but in a fervent determination to strive to please God in all things, in avoiding, as far as possible, all that would offend Him, and in praying for the increase of the glory and honour of His Son ...* (The Interior Castle, *4,1)*

Her words point us to the reason why the heart is so important to faith – it's Love's abode.

The 'Dark Night'

That was expressed and explored by her companion, John of the Cross, through his poems, especially 'The Dark Night of the Soul'. Having been accused of disobedience by his Carmelite community he was confined to a tiny, 'foul' cell high up in the wall of their monastery in Toledo. In that dark, abandoned solitude he, paradoxically, discovered the beauty and light of Christ and wrote some of the world's most sublime poetry to express the way of the soul's union with God (*via unitiva*). John's experience of external darkness reflected his inner state, which he referred to as a 'dark night' during which he experienced a painful 'purgation from sin (*via purgativa*) followed by release into spiritual freedom. He learnt what it means to simply live by faith in the faith of Jesus with whom he experienced a growing desire for union (*via illuminativa*). Such personal experience and the knowledge he gained from those who confided in him prompted him to write in detail about this journey, especially those difficult, but potentially transforming, periods.

As noted earlier, many of us find we experience times of darkness, times when even the existence of 'God' is doubted and we enter a gloomy and depressing period. But these can be of immense importance as faith is reorganized and 'God' is deconstructed in order that more of the Divine Mystery might be revealed. At such times it's important to hold on with our metaphorical fingertips to the faith we have as we may exist in apparent desolation trusting that something of importance is occurring in the soul's depths. It can be tempting to find ways of being pleasurably distracted, but we need to stay with the seismic shifts that are occurring rather than avoid them – all this is material for spiritual direction.

John's books *The Ascent of Mount Carmel* (1581–85) and *The Dark Night of the Soul* (1584–86) are treatises on his great poem, also called *The Dark Night*, and concern four 'movements' in the search for God:

- The Active Night of the Senses (*The Ascent of Mount Carmel*, Book I), during which we try to overcome those 'sins' preventing us from setting our hearts on the love of God through self-denial, prayer and nurturing the virtues (also central to Salesian spirituality), leading to the next movement.
- The Passive Night of the Senses (*The Dark Night of the Soul*, Book I), when we realize a gradual lack of delight in spiritual practices and no longer 'feel' God – doubt even God's existence. John describes this period as 'terrible', 'dark' and 'miserable', but the Spirit is at work and John

assures us of God's presence, especially when we are unaware of it.

- The Active Night of the Spirit/Soul (*The Ascent of Mount Carmel*, Books II and III) is initiated by God and invites us to live by faith, hope and love rather than depending on consoling feelings. The Passive Night of the Spirit/Soul (*Dark Night of the Soul*, Book II) concerns being drawn into further purification of desire. Only longing for God is constant as Ss. Thérèse of Lisieux and Kolkata experienced for much of their later Religious lives.

Such movements, or stages, have been compared with how, in the book of Exodus, the Hebrews (Israelites) were gradually awoken to their need for freedom from slavery in Egypt and began their long period of 'wilderness wanderings' when they were tempted to give up – yet John says that, in prayer, a longing to live by love's call remains. Finally he experienced a 'Third Movement' of entering the 'Promised Land' when the more perfect the love the deeper union in God becomes, together with a desire to live in complete accordance with the Divine (God's) Will. Of these 'movements' the second is the most important. We may sense loneliness, isolation and that awful fear we're unlovable and can react by seeking to protect our vulnerable self and look for distracting pleasures – all to 'save ourselves' – as Satan seeks to distort the truth of who we are: the beloved of our Father.

> *In you, today, he wants to relive his complete*
> *submission to his Father.*
> *It does not matter what you feel,*
> *but what he feels in you ...*
> *You and I must let him live in us*
> *and through us in the world.*
> *(St Teresa of Kolkata, 1974, to a priest*
> *suffering spiritual darkness)*

A 'Little Way'

In contrast to Teresa of Avila the life of St Thérèse of Lisieux speaks into the lived experience of many. Her short, hidden life, ending in sickness and death, led to her quickly becoming considered a saint because of the way she dealt with her sufferings, witnessing to the 'Little Way' of doing even the smallest things with love. She, too, lost awareness of Jesus' reassuring presence, but was determined to love as he loved. She knew no 'mansions' nor 'stages', but continued her life of prayer and little acts of kindness to her sisters in thanksgiving for believing, yet not feeling, God's love for her. Thérèse knew that lack of feelings couldn't mean God wasn't there – that would deny what she and so many others had experienced (it would be as if one's partner went away and, no longer feeling their presence, we decided they must no longer exist!). 'Sometimes', Thérèse wrote, 'when I'm in such a state of spiritual dryness that I can't find a single thought in my mind which will bring me close to God, I say an "Our Father" and "Hail Mary" very slowly. How they take me out of myself then, what solid satisfaction they give me!' (*Autobiography*)

Although we each have our own path, Fr Gilbert Shaw, in a sermon to the Sisters of the Love of God at Fairacres, Oxford, warned that we're 'so prone to fall in love with the means that we are in danger of forgetting the end'. A desire for mystical experience and attraction to spiritual techniques can easily blind us to the call to love. In any relationship some get no further than the initial 'movements/stages' – love concerns feelings and as long as these are satisfied, all well and good. But we can resist an invitation to be drawn deeper into a 'darker' time because it involves being stripped of our self-centredness.

A major trauma can also lead to a certain 'darkness' and requires the same patient trust that, beneath the pain, God is still present. However, some will find the journey so desolate that it seems pointless: the 'world' offers many attractions (as can some churches) and seems to get on quite well without any 'inner journey' ... yet, ultimately, the journey offers the way to our integration, our wholeness – our holiness – to what God knows we can become. About this Fr Pierre Teilhard de Chardin SJ (1881–1955) wisely wrote to his niece Marguerite Teillard-Chambon in answer to her request for advice about making a decision:

Above all, trust in the slow work of God.
We are quite naturally impatient in everything
to reach the end without delay.
We should like to skip the intermediate stages.
We are impatient of being on the way to something
unknown, something new.
And yet it is the law of all progress
that it is made by passing through
some stages of instability –
and that it may take a very long time.

Give Our Lord the benefit of believing
that his hand is leading you,
and accept the anxiety of feeling yourself
in suspense and incomplete.
(de Chardin, The Making of a Mind)

Reflections

- Read John 15 – what do you notice about this pivotal chapter?
- What does the prayer of trust say to you and what difference does faith make to the way you live and understand life?
- 'Lift up your heart to God with humble love and mean God himself, and not what you get out of him.' What benefits and difficulties are there in silence and how might the church

make use of it? Do you experience 'darkness' in prayer and, if so, what might it teach you and how might you respond?

Suggestion

Organize a meditation group and explore the wisdom of the Carmelites.

Spiritual exercise

– to deepen your relationship with Jesus in five steps:

1. **Tell** Jesus that you want to open your heart to him.
2. **Still** yourself, descend into your heart and open it to the Spirit.
3. **Recall** that Jesus opens his Heart to you and desire to receive what he gives.
4. **Respond** Margaret-Mary taught that '[devotion to the Sacred Heart] does not simply involve only rites and prayers, but rather a perfect compliance to holy virtues'.
5. **Consecrate** She also said that 'If you want to become one of [Jesus'] friends, you must offer him the sacrifice of yourself", adding that this should be repeated on the first Friday of every month.

A short liturgy

(Re)CONSECRATION OF A PARISH TO THE SACRED HEART OF JESUS (SH.3) *can be found in* Appendix 3, and *could be offered at a Sunday Eucharist during June, the month of the Sacred Heart. It can also be found here:* https://johnfrancisfriendship.co.uk/sacred-hearts.

5

Blest are the Pure in Heart

Keep your heart with all vigilance,
for from it flow the springs of life.
(Proverbs 4.23)

'How can young people keep their way pure?' asks the psalmist (119.9). 'By keeping to your words.' But many consider the purpose of Christianity is less about listening and responding to God then keeping certain rules, a view that may have become more pronounced for Anglicans when, in 1560, the Ten Commandments were ordered to be displayed on the eastern wall of parish churches, which was followed, at the Restoration of the Monarchy in 1660, by the Royal Coat of Arms being erected in a prominent position. That emphasized the link between church and state, and the role of the former in maintaining the good order of the latter which became the – literal – focus of worship.

For the psalmist, what mattered was encouraging people in following the way of *God's* laws and statutes, for that led to living a blameless life – and God's 'laws' needed to be taken into the heart (Psalm 40.8). It wasn't just a matter of 'keeping the rules', but letting the heart be formed by God's commands: 'You desire truth in the inward being; therefore teach me wisdom in my secret heart' (Psalm 51.6). Unfortunately the quest for 'right living', for 'purity', can easily ignore the need to practise mercy and compassion and become all-consuming and puritanical, leading to the heart being poisoned by pride, exclusivity, judgementalism, condemnation and fragmentation.

But one young man who kept all the rules sensed there was still 'more' he needed to discover (Matthew 19.16f.). On questioning Jesus he learnt that perfection required him to 'go, sell, give', a response requiring abandonment to love, generosity and selflessness. It's a lifetime's loving work which, as Jesus' apparitions to Margaret-Mary remind us (Chapter 3), requires these basic ingredients:

- Sorrow for sin and repentance by confession, contrition and the promise of amendment.
- Lively, not tepid, faith (cf. Revelation 3.8–16).
- A real desire to love Jesus, especially in his sufferings, and detachment from self-concern and pride.
- Recollection: 'perfect devotion to the Sacred Heart is a continuous exercise of love for Jesus' (Croiset, *The Devotion to the Sacred Heart*, p. 102).

If the heart doesn't 'hear' this call and we're not committed to its conversion even our best intentions can be corrupted. Any involved with 'conversion' practices or 'church planting' should remember this because it's easy to fall prey to darker forces connected with competitiveness, power and success. But if the Sacred Heart governs and guides us, it will have a profound effect on how we express the faith: Jesus doesn't want to dominate or control, but help our heart be moulded by his.

> *Your task is not to seek for love, but merely to seek and find all the barriers within yourself that you have built against it and embrace them. (Rumi, 13th-century Persian poet and Sufi mystic)*

Purity of heart

This call to 'go deeper' with God will involve
facing Jesus' declaration: 'Blessed are the pure
of heart, for they will see God' because 'seeing'
– at-oneness with God – involves the cleansing
of one's heart as Mark's Gospel reminds us:
'… it is from within, from the human heart, that evil intentions come' (7.21). The Hebrew scriptures record how Moses
discovered that intimacy with God required purification
(Exodus 19) and while that concerned physical washing it's
more important, as Jesus said, to cleanse the heart, some of
his greatest denunciations being aimed at those who focused
on externals while ignoring their own inner life (Matthew
23.26f.).

The title of this chapter comes from a famous hymn written
by John Keble (1792–1866), a formative and creative leader
of the Anglo-Catholic movement, which concerned both
personal sanctity and social activity. It also points to Jesus'
own struggles in the wilderness as the purity of his Heart was
tested. The Sacred Heart reminds us that the call to address
corruption, individual and social, can be costly, but must be
governed by compassion. Christianity involves the purifying
of our humanity so we can come to that fullness of life promised by God; it involves all we do, how we live and, in that,
the heart of who we are either aids or hinders our efforts –
which is why images of the Sacred Heart include symbols of
blood, fire and thorns.

Purification of heart, through which we acquire humility,
and every blessing that comes from above, consists simply
in our not letting evil thoughts enter the soul. (Hesychios
the Priest, On Watchfulness and Holiness, *p. 193)*

A HEALTHY HEART

'By encouraging devotion to the Heart of Jesus, (we exhort) believers to open themselves to the mystery of God and of his love and to allow themselves to be transformed by it ... it is still a fitting task for Christians to continue to deepen their relationship with the Heart of Jesus, in such a way as to revive their faith in the saving love of God and to welcome him ever better into their lives.'
(Pope Benedict XVI, 50th Anniversary of the Encyclical, Haurietis Aquas, 2006)

Walking across the heath near to where I live for the Eucharist often involves encountering groups of 30-somethings engaged in various physical exercises. St Paul knew about these and admitted (rather counter-culturally these days) that they were of 'some value' (1 Timothy 4.8a), but I wonder if those training their bodies ever consider 'spiritual exercises' which Paul says are 'valuable in every way'? Care for the body is important, but if we neglect our inner life then our well-being will only be skin (or muscle) deep – something the Desert Elders knew and about which they left a treasury of wisdom.

Attentiveness to love

The book of Proverbs says this about developing a healthy heart: 'Keep your heart with all vigilance, for from it flow the springs of life' (4.23). Such attentiveness requires a certain stillness and willingness to listen to the movements deep within lest any of the passions begin to drive us and overwhelm the virtues we're to nurture.

Awareness of, and response to, being loved also aids the heart's health and, if there's been a lack of such in the past, some may wonder what 'love' actually means. So it might help to reflect on Paul's description in 1 Corinthians 13.4f. It can also help to spend a specific period of time with the intention of really noticing all the different ways in which people express love for us – the passer-by who offers a smile, the kindness of a stranger or embrace of a friend – it might not always be in ways we want, but awareness that we *do* experience aspects of love, even if it's the beauty of a radiant sunset, will be of great help. Some will have been so hurt in childhood or adolesence that they've erected protective walls around their heart, and allowing Love to trickle through any fissures to cleanse the spoiled 'cave' of its history will be risky. To do so will require courage and humility but, despite any early life-traumas, there comes a time when we need to accept being part of the 'walking wounded' – for just as Christ's Heart was scarred so it is with and through our wounds that we are to live – and love.

It usually requires time for this realization to occur, just as we may need time to move beyond the need to please others, earn respect, approval or feel we're being judged and 'found out' – by God and others. It may take years before we can sit openly in God's presence as one sits with a lover or friend and begin to ask what God wants of us ... deeper conversion? ... movement beyond needing the felt-presence of God? ... more perfect faith, hope and love? ... to accept suffering with Christ? ... to have the courage to 'stand in (God's) presence and serve (him)' among the disadvantaged and oppressed, as well as the Liturgy, as one of the Eucharistic Prayers declares.

How does God view me?

> '... the LORD does not see as mortals see; they look on the
> outward appearance, but the LORD looks on the heart.'
> (1 Samuel 16.7b)

Some have been brought up to believe that love is condi-
tional on behaviour. At times we're prevented from realizing
love by something as simple (and profoundly damaging) as
pride which, haughtily, dismisses the need for that humility
to know we can't save ourselves, can't 'earn' more love than
God already has for us. And to realize that, in spite of our
sins – our hidden faults, blemishes and failures – we're still
loved by God who entered the flesh we inhabit and so views
us from the perspective of a material heart into which were
breathed spiritual Energies (Genesis 2.7).

To draw close to the Sacred Heart involves becoming
sensitive to ourselves as loved sinners. As this occurs we
need to know that Christ's Heart suffered and find ways to
understand how we're to 'complet[e] what is lacking in [his]
afflictions for the sake of his body ... the church' (Colossians
1.24). This can cause confusion and pain and will probably
conflict with any specific desire for that 'peace' many hope
religion will provide. Yet such peace can only come as the
heart is cleansed of sin, desires to live out of the Divine Will
and lays its burdens on Christ.

Testing of hearts

Just as Jesus discovered in the wilderness, once the heart is
set on God it will be tested to help increase its desire. So
don't be surprised if (when) you lose awareness of God's love
while becoming more conscious of your disordered desires.
Rather than faith leading to a problem-free life we might consider that if our hands and hearts felt satisfied we may desire

nothing more. Looking back over my life I recognize that God invites me to walk by faith, not certainty; love, not security. That poverty of spirit which Jesus said is blessed concerns the way through which we must struggle and, failing and falling, start again by God's grace and our humility.

RENEWING THE HEART

A new heart I will give you, and a new spirit I will put within you; and I will remove from your body the heart of stone and give you a heart of flesh. (Ezekiel 36.26)

The promise of a 'new heart' isn't a matter of surgery, but of the Spirit's refashioning. Any 'hardness' is softened through practising the virtues – faith, hope, love, the pursuit of justice and peace, temperance, courage and wisdom – as we constantly struggle with the lure of the passions and vices: 'I entreat you not to leave your heart unguarded' (Isaac the Syrian, *Philokalia*, 'On Guarding the Intellect'). We may not consider ourselves great sinners but, stop for a moment and ask yourself, do I secretly relish someone being put down? Or want to be the centre of attention? Am I greedy ... abusive ... envious ...? Do I tell little lies? Is it 'my way or the highway'? If criticized does my heart become 'hot within me' and 'burst into flame' causing me to speak out of anger in the presence of the 'wicked' (Psalm 39.4f.)?

None of us are perfect. When St Peter saw the miracle of the great catch of fish (Luke 5.1f.) he knew himself to be in the presence of One to whom his response was: 'Leave me, Lord, for I am a sinful man.' Standing before the purity of holiness our heart can recognize its *im*purity and the process of cleansing it can be painful, but the more it is 'purified' the more God's love can find a home in it. The lesson we need to learn is to have the humility to live with our 'light' *and* 'darkness' (you cannot have one without the other) while giving our attention to the former.

The Great Deceiver

> *Within the heart are unfathomable depths. It is but a small vessel and yet dragons and lions are there, and poisonous creatures and all the treasures of wickedness; rough, uneven paths are there, and gaping chasms. There likewise is God, there are the angels, there life and the Kingdom, there light and the Apostles, the heavenly cities and the treasures of grace: all things are there.*
> *(Abba Macarius, 300–91, Homilies)*

However, a heart given to corruption can attract others. Satan appeals to our 'darker' side and will be pleased when we feel enabled to indulge in corrupt behaviour. I know terms like 'Satan', 'evil spirits', etc. can be used to deflect our responsibility – 'it was the devil made me do it!' – but it appears that *something* beyond definition can appropriate the heart leading it to act in ways regarded as 'evil', something addressed by the ancient prayer (the Embolism) after the Our Father during the Eucharist: 'Deliver us, Lord, from every evil …'

Secularized societies can find it hard to acknowledge the existence of that which our ancestors named Satan, the Father of Lies, the Adversary, the Great Deceiver. Yet it seems humanity still has an Enemy and we can find negative, life-denying forces appealing, forces that prefer not being named (and thus acknowledged) so their work of debasing individuals, communities and nations can continue unhindered. The ego of individuals whose hearts are deceived will want to dominate and they'll regress to being demanding babies unable to understand Christ's call. Unfortunately some churches collude with this by promoting success, idolizing wealth and seeking unbridled power while giving lip-service to Christ-like compassion. The call for the heart's conversion to his love may irritate them because they've lost touch with their soul – no wonder Jesus observes: 'what will it profit them if they gain the whole world but forfeit their life?' (Matthew 16.26).

> *Your decrees are my inheritance for ever;*
> *they are the joy of my heart.*
> *I incline my heart to perform your statutes*
> *for ever, to the end.*
> *I hate the double-minded,*
> *but I love your law.*
> *(Psalm 119.111–113)*

Sufism and the heart

In recognizing these corrupting forces Sufi Islam speaks of purifying or 'polishing' the heart: 'Dear friend,' advised al-Ghazali (c.1058–1111) in *The Secret of Secrets*, 'your heart is a polished mirror. You must wipe it clean of the veil of dust that has gathered upon it, because it is destined to reflect the light of divine secrets.' The more 'polished' our heart the more of the divine it can reflect: 'Go, sweep out the dwelling-room of your heart', said Mahmoud Shabistarî (1288–1340) in his poem 'The chamber of your heart', 'pre-pare it to be the abode and home of the Beloved: when you go out He will come in. Within you, when you are free from self, He will show His Beauty.' Jesus warned that this polishing – cleansing – requires constant attention (Matthew 12.44f.) if anything of the Divine is to be reflected. Sufism recommends two methods of 'polishing': remembrance of God and recog-nizing and gaining control over the 'lower self'.

God placed the heart within the cavity of the human chest,
and it belongs to God alone. No one can have any claim
on it. God holds the heart between two of his fingers, and
no one is allowed access to it: not angel, nor prophet, nor
any created being in the whole of creation. God alone
turns it as he wishes. Within the heart God placed the
Knowledge of Him and He lit it with the divine light ...
by this light He gave the heart eyes to see. (Al-Hakim
al-Tirmidhi, c.755–869, K. al-riyada-we-adab al-nafs,
1947)

'There is a polish for everything that takes away rust; and the
polish of the heart is *Dhikr* of Allah' (Abu al-Darda, ob.652,
Shu'ab al-Imān, 503). Like the Jesus Prayer or Litany of the
Sacred Heart (Appendix 4), *dhikr* are ritual prayers offered
for the purpose of glorifying God throughout the day and
bringing attention back to the heart whereby Lover and
beloved can be united: 'I have become the One I love, and
the One I love has become me! We are two spirits infused in
a (single) body' (extract from a poem by Mansour al-Hallaj,
858–922).

Much earlier Paul had written of the importance of praying
without ceasing, leading, by the fifth century, to orthodox
monks practising a life of 'hesychasm' (stillness/contempla-
tion through uninterrupted prayer). In this 'prayer of the
heart', the Jesus Prayer is considered paramount because it
is a prayer that, beginning on the lips, is to be prayed in time
with one's breathing in the silence of the heart.

Until we have seen the light of Christ, we cannot really
see our sins. So long as the room is in darkness ... we do
not notice the dirt; but when we bring a powerful light
into the room ... we can distinguish every speck of dust.
So it is with the room of our soul. (Kallistos Ware, The
Inner Kingdom, pp. 46–7. Quoted with permission)

HUMILITY

The sacrifice acceptable to God is a broken spirit;
a broken and contrite heart, O God,
you will not despise.
(Psalm 51.17)

This polishing concerns the primary virtue of humility: 'Learn from me,' said Jesus, 'for I am gentle and humble in heart.' His humble heart was the focus and inspiration for Francis de Sales who, it's said, created a 'tapestry of love' woven by a 'world of hearts'. There's nothing to fear about humility; it leads to our greatness because it concerns the ground of our being where we discover aspects of ourselves, some of which might easily be overlooked.

This matter of being 'emptied' reflects that assertion of John the Baptist: 'he (Jesus) must increase, but I must decrease' (John 3.30). This can be difficult in a culture often preoccupied with 'self' – self-image, self-promotion, self-improvement, self-concern, 'selfies' – forgetting that wisdom says, get over your-self! Have we become so *self*-absorbed that we've forgotten the need for self-transcendence and the wisdom of self-denial – the primacy of love for the other? The nature of the Heart that draws us isn't self-centred but full of mercy and compassion calling us to leave self behind while attending to the Other. In his book *The Imitation of Christ*, St Thomas à Kempis (1380–1471) wrote:

Had you but once entered perfectly into the Heart of Jesus, and tasted something of His burning love, you would care nothing for your own gain or loss; for the love of Jesus causes a man to regard himself very humbly.

The true, inward lover of Jesus and the Truth, who is free from inordinate desires, can turn freely to God, rise above self, and joyfully rest in God. (Ch. 26)

This seems of particular importance to the vocation of ministers of the gospel. Called into a unique relationship with the Lord it's easy for them, because of their role within a religious (or secular) community, to get carried away, puffed up or blind to the extent some speak of a 'career in the church' or talk about 'what *I* want to do with *my* vocation'. We all need a healthy sense of who we are – a healthy ego – but it's easy to forget that it's Christ's call to which we must attend: if our ego begins to dominate that can have devastating consequences as we see in some families, nations – and the church. So it is that those words of John the Baptist about increasing and decreasing need to be held before the eye of our heart because they speak of the necessity of our lives being built on the foundation of humility so that any pride we experience doesn't blind us to our actual state – sinners in need of a saviour.

If you see a young man climbing toward heaven by his own will, grab his foot and pull him down, for it will be for his own good. (Stewart, World of the Desert Fathers, *p. 37)*

But Satan will always be on the lookout for ways to encourage us to 'increase' … No wonder the Orthodox realize the importance of the Jesus Prayer; humility doesn't come easily and may not be comfortable, but it keeps us human. We need to pray for the grace to welcome our faults being – painfully – pointed out while seeing another praised and elevated yet hopefully, and possibly after a struggle, rejoicing for them. Jesus reminds us to take the log out of our own eye before looking at the splinter in another's and was constantly attacking the pride of Jewish religious leaders. This is all part of the way of 'decreasing' shown through that parable often called 'the Prodigal's Return' as he comes to the truth about himself (humility). Realizing that what he'd set his heart upon has led to ruin and having lost his original innocence he repented – turned back to his father: humility asks, upon what is my heart set?

The opposite of humility is, of course, that most basic vice – the self-idolatry of over-weening pride. At a time when 'greatness' is lauded as aspirational Jesus tells us it concerns the humility required to become like a little child (Matthew 8.3). That's not about childishness but having that vulnerability without which the heart becomes guarded, hardened and walled-up. That is what we see in Christ who '... emptied himself, taking the form of a slave, being born in human likeness. And being found in human form, he humbled himself and became obedient to ... death on a cross' (Philippians 2.7–8).

Self-awareness

While valuing the virtues there have been times I've angrily reacted to something said because my self-image has been punctured, my mask shattered; the struggle between self-will and humility is long, hard and – at times – confusing as the Holy Spirit coaxes us to say 'thy will be done' and we discover that, as Dante declared, 'in his will is our peace' (*Paradiso*, Canto 3, 85f.). It's only when pride collapses and we have the humility to admit 'I'm lost!' and turn, quite simply, to Christ's Heart that we discover, unexpectedly, a deep sense of freedom. A veil seems removed, tears may flow, we sense a fresh and greater clarity and an upsurge of love emerges as the heart surrenders to God.

Humility develops as we see ourselves in the light of Christ who, for love's sake, descended into the depths to 'find' us

(1 Peter 3.18f. – which is why Holy Saturday is so important – just as God sought out our primal parents. It's the antidote to the elevation of the 'self' and the gateway to repentance by which the heart is cleansed: abiding in the Sacred Heart provides the foundation on which to build our lives and live them to God's greater glory. That doesn't mean we won't get things wrong or that the heart won't be love's home, times when it's easy for another – one who is the dark shadow of love's brightness – to take possession. There'll be occasions when we say or do something that, unintentionally, causes profound distress to another. Initially unaware of this I've felt shocked and revolted on realizing the consequences of something I've said or done: suddenly I see myself through this particular prism and any self-worth I have is shattered. What's revealed isn't pleasant and I wonder if this is how others see me or sense that 'if they only realized what I'm *really* like ...' But, '[i]t is not constant thought of their sins, but the vision of the holiness of God that makes the saints aware of their own sinfulness' (Metropolitan Anthony of Sourozh, *The Essence of Prayer*, p. 9).

In *The Hidden Man of the Heart* by Archimandrite Zacharias the Orthodox monk Fr Sophrony reminds us that the best (and more difficult) response to this awareness is to humble ourselves before the offended person, not becoming upset or antagonistic – but 'even offering a real smile' (p. 79). Yet what often happens is that we seek for something negative about them; or we might turn from the revelation, wallow in self-loathing or pity and simply feed the heart's desolation which the 'evil spirit' wants to stir up. *Or ...* we could recognize the gift offered by the experience, humbly grasp the opportunity to accept that this is only an aspect of who we are, be contrite for our actions, realize this as an opportunity for amendment and confess our sin.

Compunction – the 'prick' of conscience

Once we see the truth that we've become prey to the Evil spirit we can begin to live with 'compunction'. Unlike guilt, which can haunt us, compunction is that encouraging 'prick of conscience' warning us not to sin again, but to nurture the virtues necessary for living a Christ-like life, for regaining the nobility of our true God-like nature.

God remains faithful and never forsakes us, but waits, like the Prodigal's compassionate father, for our (re)turning – and runs to meet us. It takes humility to accept criticism (and not retaliate), admit mistakes, be prepared to be viewed in a bad light and seek forgiveness. Moments of illumination are to be welcomed – 'yes, I see what you're pointing to – thank you – and, by the grace of God, I'll seek to amend my life'. While apologies are, probably, appropriate the oft-ignored Confessional (Appendix 5) is the place to own sin as we pray to cultivate whatever graces will help growth into greater Christ-likeness.

Although much of this might seem to speak more to introverts than extraverts we all need to familiarize ourselves with what lies within else we'll never become integrated, something not aided if cultures – secular or religious – disregard the need to cultivate the inner being. As we turn our attention inward we also face this matter of 'sin', which is more than a matter of having 'broken the rules' or not abiding by what the Bible (or church) 'teaches'. While biblical literalists or church traditionalists can focus on 'rules' these can prevent us, as Jesus said, recognizing the 'weightier matters of the law' (Mathew 23.23) and the effect of such blindness to the primacy of love is seen everywhere. This becomes acute when fundamentalist, Puritanical, culture-based religion mixes with nationalism and individuals, churches or nations begin to be idolized. Faith that has become attached to tribal myths needs confronting (and converting) by the challenging Heart of Jesus.

METANOIA

Yet even now, says the LORD,
return to me with all your heart,
with fasting, with weeping, and with mourning;
rend your hearts and not your clothing.
(Joel 2.12–13)

Consumer culture sets out to convince us that all we need for our contentment is readily available – at a price. But Holy Wisdom tells us that conversion of the heart is the foundation of that life to which we're called. Some hesitate and never begin this process, finding the thought of engaging in it unattractive or, recognizing its benefits, begin but fall away – and if they start again they may be unable to embrace the process wholeheartedly. A few, knowing it'll be costly and involve failures, press on believing that, by the grace of God and the Spirit's aid, however painful the process this Heart-to-heart call needs ongoing attention.

Wash yourselves; make yourselves clean;
remove the evil of your doings
from before my eyes;
cease to do evil,
learn to do good;
seek justice,
rescue the oppressed,
defend the orphan,
plead for the widow.
Come now, let us argue it out,
says the LORD:
though your sins are like scarlet,

they shall be like snow;
though they are red like crimson,
they shall become like wool.
(Isaiah 1.16–18)

Repentance – restoring the image

Most of us try to lead a good life, yet, 'If we say that we have no sin, we deceive ourselves, and the truth is not in us ...' (1 John 1.8). Our need for this constant conversion – refocusing – through repentance is termed, in Greek, *metanoia*. We're to 'put to death' whatever leads us astray in order to be clothed in the new self.

For some this seems to happen quite suddenly: they feel swept up in Christ but may not realize it's only the beginning of a life-long process. To think we've arrived when we've only been redirected can result in feelings of desolation or disillusionment when the initial buzz wears off unless we're helped to realize there's a long journey ahead before final at-oneness with God. We need to live with that poverty of spirit which doesn't seek riches as we make the gift of self to Christ, no matter how we feel, and commit ourselves to gospel living. This is why the Religious Life, with its evangelical counsels of poverty, chastity and obedience, or the monastic vows of stability, *conversio morum* and obedience, has so much to teach us about living in the Heart of Christ.

My child, if you accept my words
and treasure up my commandments within you,
making your ear attentive to wisdom
and inclining your heart to understanding;
then you will ... find the knowledge of God.
(Proverbs 2.1–2, 5)

Confession – reconciliation

Life in Christ is marked by Baptism and renewed by the grace (spiritual aid) offered through feeding on his sacramental Body and Blood. Yet still we will fall, need to repent and amend our life which is why Christ gave us the valuable sacrament of Confession (John 20.22f.). It's hard to own our sin before another and many shy away, but since the times of the Desert Elders who sought a radical transformation of their hearts through a life of repentance, the quest for at-oneness with God has been known to be associated with this cleansing and healing sacrament. It is not only used when we commit serious sins but as a regular means of *metanoia*, for it offers that grace by which our lives are changed as we face – admit – the ways in which 'me' and 'mine' obscure the two great commandments and damage both our humanity and the image of God in which we're made.

Anyone wanting to deepen their relationship with Jesus will find this sacrament of great benefit and, by virtue of their ordination, every priest is charged with offering it – although some prefer not to and others don't feel skilled in its practice. And because Christ is the one to whom we come through the ministry of the confessor, the confessional is a place of complete confidentiality which the priest is bound to maintain by law – what's said there stays there.

I know some won't approach the confessional because they fear experiencing shame which, unlike guilt, concerns who we are rather than what we've done or omitted to do. But this aspect of compunction can be healthy – it indicates that the heart has been affected. Others say, 'God forgives me; I don't need to confess to a priest', but the humility required to open ourselves to another (also held in Jesus' Heart) enables the words of absolution to be heard in the soul's depths. Sadly, the value of this gift isn't always explained.

The sacrifice acceptable to God is a broken spirit;
a broken and contrite heart, O God, you will not despise.
(Psalm 51.17)

REMEMBER – YOU ARE IN THE HEART OF GOD

There will always be times when we feel far from God, when we want give up or feel lost or exhausted, which is when it's important to stop and 'remember your first love'. Do you realize you're loved in the depth of your being? It's something we may not always feel … but do we *believe* it – 'know' it, allow the fact to permeate our intuition? Do we relish that just as we might stop and consider the wonder and joy of our partner's love (if we have one) and let it speak into us?

From time to time I find nothing more wonderful than doing just that – to stop and consider how, with all my faults, I'm loved by *this* person who has honoured me by sharing his life with me, has entrusted me with a share in *his* heart. But if you don't have such a partner then consider this – if others *are* loved in that way, how much more glorious must be God's love for you – and all people. Sadly some clearly consider their god is full of condemnation, but the Sacred Heart is, quite simply, an ocean of Love.

… what God is waiting for is not a right conclusion
about a matter
but for our suppleness in falling into his hands
for him to work in us.
(Sr Benedicta Ward SLG,
Discernment: A Rare Bird, *p. 10f.)*

Reflections

- Recall those dispositions Margaret-Mary said were necessary for life in Christ:
  - a lively, not tepid, faith;
  - a real desire to love Jesus, especially in his sufferings, and a detachment from self-concern and pride;
  - recollection: 'perfect devotion to the Sacred Heart is a continuous exercise of love for Jesus'.

  How do these speak into your own faith? How do you express them? Which need greater attention, and why?
- Theophan the Recluse graphically referred to the act of confession to a priest as one of 'vomiting out' everything that poisons us (*Turning the Heart to God*, p. 117).
  - What might help someone make use of the sacrament of Confession?

Spiritual exercise

At a time when physical exercise is encouraged churches might consider offering 'Spiritual Exercises', some of which have already been suggested. The following could also be used by individuals or groups.

Ignatius Loyola was concerned to free the heart from any life-denying desires in order to choose that which will lead us to God. One of the 'Exercises' he offered is known as *The Two Standards*, the context of which is a battleground where Satan and Jesus face each other beneath their 'standards' (flags). The following could be used as a group or individual exercise to help recognize, in the depths of the heart, the draw of both and the consequence of giving them attention.

Method

First, become prayerfully centred. Then imagine looking over a great plain on one side of which stands Jesus and his saints, those who reveal his love and want us to join in kingdom-living, and on the other is 'Satan' surrounded by his forces whom he directs to convert the world. It can be helpful to see these troops gathered beneath their own standard/flag.

Imagine who or what today might represent Satan, the 'Great Tempter'. Consider what they want of you and how they tempt you. Ignatius speaks of the enticements of wealth, honour and pride (*has anything changed …?*). Notice what touches your heart – and consider the consequences. Ignatius said that the pride associated with this temptation – 'I've made it and don't need God' – leads 'to all the other vices'. How might this still be true?

Then look at Jesus. What 'forces' does he have? What is his appeal – his message for the world? What does he say about the treasure of spiritual poverty as opposed to pride? Ignatius says we should pray for the grace to desire 'poverty as opposed to riches; insults or contempt as opposed to worldly honour, and humility as opposed to pride' – how do you respond?

Finally, compare the two, considering how they might affect the way you would live – and make notes (or share in group discussion).

6

Compassionate Hearts

Be mindful of your mercy, O LORD,
and of your steadfast love,
for they have been from of old.
(Psalm 25.6)

Often we're exposed to great suffering through means of the media and our heart is moved. Christ certainly calls us to be compassionate and to take action on behalf of the poor, marginalized and victimized, but there'll be occasions when we feel overwhelmed by the sheer scale of suffering. In 1894, moved by the appalling conditions in London's East End, three Anglican priests – Frs Andrew (Henry) Hardy, James Adderley and Henry Chappel – realized a call to address this through going to live among and serving the poor in Plaistow, East London. Taking vows of poverty, chastity and obedience they named themselves the Society of Divine Compassion (SDC), a title expressing the charism of their new Order which they dedicated to St Francis, our Lady – and the Sacred Heart.

For decades the community witnessed to Christ's compassionate Heart and their impact on the East End and farther afield was immense. At about the same time, Fr Arthur Shearly Cripps (1869–1952) arrived in Southern Rhodesia where, because of his compassion for the black population, he was described as 'our modern St Francis', a vocation he expressed in his poem 'The Death of St Francis':

I felt his Heart to beat within my heart.
It seemed He lent his Sacred Heart to me:
One moment did I know His wish, His work,
As if my own they were, and knew with them
The worm-like weakness of my wasted life,
My service worthless to win back His world
(Sharp Sister Faintness knits dark brows at me),
And o'er her shoulder looks sweet Sister Death,
Holding a glass my last hour's sands run down.
(Fr Arthur Shearly Cripps, Africa: Verses*)*

Jesu, thou art all compassion

Most great religions attest to God's compassionate nature. Throughout the Hebrew scriptures there are references to compassion – for example, the story of the binding of Isaac for sacrifice culminates in a ram being substituted revealing that God did not require human sacrifice; the spilling of Jesus' blood was the consequence of his merciful and compassionate love which had caused him to weep at the grave of his friend Lazarus. He healed crowds and individuals and when asked 'who is my neighbour?' placed a despised foreigner at the heart of his teaching (Luke 10.25–37).

Hard-wired into us from primitive times is a fear of the foreigner, the stranger – the 'other' – yet our faith is rooted in One who, with his parents, experienced the plight of being refugees. It constantly refers to the need to care for the 'alien' in our midst (e.g. Leviticus 19.34) but, sadly, those whose hearts have become corrupted choose to dismiss this call, while politicians can play on our primal fears in an effort to gain and maintain their power. In that they're supported by the right-wing media whose power to misinform and misshape the heart by appealing to our 'darker' nature can be, superficially, more attractive than the Word of God. Christians can also be affected by the way some church leaders use particular scriptural verses to uphold prejudices. Taking as an example that incident in Genesis 19, where Sodom is destroyed because the 'men of the city' demand to 'know' the angels/men whom Lot, an 'alien', had invited to stay in his house, they claim this indicates that homosexuality is sinful in God's eyes. Yet this isn't a story about (male) homosexuality (and consequent acceptance of female rape); it's an account of God's judgement on those who don't show hospitality towards strangers – who lack compassion.

Empathy, suffering and compassion

It was divine compassion that brought Christ into the world, a compassion apparent even during the last moments of his life when he promised that the penitent thief would enter Paradise. It was Jesus' compassionate Heart that angered the conservative leaders who began viewing him as a threat.

Compassion arises from our ability to empathize with suffering as we step out of our shoes into another's and, as such, is a mark of our humanity. Although that can be challenging, the way our heart can be moved to help another makes this one of the most important and beautiful of all human virtues, one needed if we're to overcome that hatred that affects individuals, groups and society, leading to hard-heartedness and the evil of nationalism. In 1837 it was compassion that moved the young Marian Rebecca Hughes to begin caring for the disadvantaged, leading her to become the first Anglican since the Reformation to live publicly under the vows of poverty, chastity and obedience. Many followed where she led, showing that being a disciple of the Crucified isn't about living stress-free 'peaceful' lives but accepting that Christ calls us, by his grace, to 'bear one another's burdens' (Galatians 6.2).

Such a witness to a radical understanding of the gospel and its call to compassion shows how it can be shaped by an awareness of Christ's Heart (cf. John 8.39f.). Often sharing in the life of the marginalized and embracing those vows, Religious show how our faith is rooted in certain social principles as revealed by the life of the first Christian community which grew as they transcended their Jewish exclusivity.

Love of the Sacred Heart is inseparable from compassion and, although our hearts aren't large or strong enough to carry the world's troubles, the Heart of Jesus offers to enfold them and is a place to rest and lay our cares; maybe this is the reason why some who struggle with life find being tattooed with the Sacred Heart connects with their deepest needs.

Many of Jesus' encounters show that, being in touch with his feelings, he was able to connect with others in their need while not being driven or ruled by those feelings. It's easy to allow our heart to be manipulated by others which is why, even between the hearts of lovers, a certain distance needs to be kept – we aren't to merge with them; union involves partnership not sublimation.

As the source of compassion, it's Jesus' Heart that must inform our views rather than any political dogma or narrow religious beliefs. And when the needs of the poor, refugees and vulnerable appear to threaten our standard of living then the psalmist's cry will always be a challenge:

> ... *how long will your hearts be closed,*
> *will you love what is futile and seek what is false?*
> *(Psalm 4.2)*

Unfortunately charismatic leaders can appeal to our self-centred, controlling instincts and become false messiahs whose creeds may have a superficial appeal but run counter to the gospel. Jesus warns us about blind guides who 'strain out a gnat but swallow a camel', his call to compassion confronting any desire to judge others by ever-narrowing norms rather than that mercy and love that must inform the heart. Compassion means we have to risk being open and vulnerable to another, and the pain (and possible confusion) that comes as our hearts are stretched.

Suffering and sanctity

In his book *The Hidden Man of the Heart* Archimandrite Zacharias (Spiritual Father at the Orthodox Monastery of St John the Baptist in Essex) reminds us that unless pain informs our heart we cannot offer anything of value to the world, and the 'richer' someone's experience of suffering the more powerful their witness can be. There's a particular danger that the church is seen as being – and offering – a place of comfortable conformity, with 'spirituality' concerning pleasant feelings and warm glows. Yet the Heart of Christ shows how sanctity involves transformative suffering and the spirituality of the Sacred Heart reveals a pathway through loss and darkness. Living with suffering needs great patience as Christ enables that transformation to occur: 'When we come to know every aspect of life in Christ in all its depth even the very abyss of hell', Zaccharias writes, 'then Christ's resurrection expands our knowledge, and our ministry can be meaningful and fruitful' (p. 197).

No one is free from suffering. There's the 'everyday' sort – headaches, minor injuries, viruses, name-calling, etc. – but many suffer from corrupted hearts driving people to dominate, abuse, control and succeed (at all costs). Others are profoundly affected by the suffering of those they love: parents will experience terrible anguish when their child hurts and we empathize with the heartfelt cry – 'why?' Could a supposedly loving God allow such things? Yet, as we discover through the book of Job, this can mark the start of wrestling with the paradox of being human, a paradox expressed through the Passion, death and resurrection of Christ: for the depths of love are revealed by our compassionate response to suffering.

Over the years I've listened to people speak of encounters with extreme suffering and noticed how some tell of the 'gifts' they've received. They've drawn closer to those they love, or realize in a more powerful way their ability to be compassionate and merciful. Some talk of a sense of standing before the 'doorway' of a mystery through which they feel drawn, one connected with the virtue of hope – not the optimistic 'it'll be fine in the end', but something wedded to faith in the goodness of God which 'surpasses all understanding' (Philippians, 4.7) for, as Julian of Norwich taught, with God all shall be well.

It was the crucified Son who cried from his Heart, 'It is accomplished' before giving up his spirit and who, at his Ascension, took his wounds into the Heart of the Trinity; wounds that, according to the prayer at the preparation of the Paschal Candle at the Easter Vigil, are 'holy' and 'glorious'. After the Candle is incised with the cross, five grains of incense are inserted into its soft wax, symbolizing those places where Jesus' body was pierced, with the words: '(1) By his holy (2) and glorious wounds (3) may Christ the Lord (4) guard us (5) and keep us.' They affirm the sanctity of these openings – including the wound into his Heart – enabling his prayer of self-offering to ascend like incense, revealing how accepting and living with woundedness *can* be an important means of intercession and maturing. While this doesn't 'explain' suffering it shows how it can be a paradoxical mystery awaiting disclosure.

Heart of Jesus, be my peace
Thy wounded side my home
Thy broken feet my following
Thy pierced hands my guiding
Thy crown of thorns my exceeding rich reward
Thy cross my daily toil
Thou knowest all, O my God

Thou knowest my wretchedness
Thou knowest that I love thee.
(*Gilbert Shaw,* A Pilgrim's Book of Prayers*)*

The Father and the suffering Son

There are times when, like Job, all we hold dear is taken from us for no apparent reason and we wonder whether there's any point in living. Easy answers from 'Job's comforters' can add to a sense that no one really understands or appreciates what we're going through and it's easy to be sucked into a whirlpool of desolation. Yet, beneath the pain, Christianity affirms that we're held by a loving God who cannot abandon us and whose ultimate will is for our good. We won't, necessarily, 'feel' God's compassion, but it's crucial to hold it as a fact until it *can* be known. One of the ways this happens is by following the command to love, not least when we may not feel that *we* are loved. We might rage against perceived injustices, but if love for the other (even the 'enemy') ceases to be our desire then we're on the way to being lost; redemptive love is the 'yeast' making us whole while affecting the deepest levels of the world's pain.

To the Heart

I
It was hard going, hard
daggers of dust cutting
into eyes and soft skin.
Our hearts longed to divide,
to turn back down the broad
track of distracted dreams,
crossing to avoid those
lying by the roadside.

2

Something kept us going:
deep calling out to deep,
pulling on the soul's strings
and loving our longing.
We felt our hearts soften
like grass beneath the dew,
like grace beneath the skin –
and the air sang for joy.

3

At the end of the road
a woman wrapped herself
in a cloak woven of
sunlight and whispered prayers.
'Come,' she said and led us
to the table of stone,
where one like us broke bread
and washed our aching soles.

4

His heart was the sky's arc,
the caverns of the earth;
a chalice forged by love,
filled to overflowing;
a shelter from the cruel
lie that we are not loved.
'Sit by the fire,' he said
'and let your heart be filled.'
(Steven Shakespeare SMMS)

Darkness and desolation

During times of suffering it's understandable that some look
for practices that answer a need to feel God's comforting,

compassionate presence. Absence of such a feeling can lead to despair when we might be tempted to abandon the journey with Christ altogether or turn to whatever might numb the pain. As right as it is to sing 'Rejoice in the Lord always ...' (Philippians 4.4) it often needs to begin with an act of the will, especially if the heart hurts or is divided – or is asleep.

Such experiences can feel desolating ... life is empty and the temptation to flee can be great – how could a compassionate God allow this? But it can be important to stay there and, with patient faith and love, ask to be aware of God *in* that place – for such inner 'howling wilderness wastes' (Deuteronomy 32.10) can veil mysteries. From at least the third century some left the bustling cities of Egypt, Palestine, Syria, etc. to face the 'demons' and 'phantoms' found in in the desert (apathy, fear, sexual desire, etc.) taking the light of Christ into places symbolizing the heart's emptiness.

ANGER • BLAME • MERCY

The Heart of Jesus is the ultimate symbol of God's mercy.
But it is not an imaginary symbol;
it is a real symbol which represents the centre,
the source from which salvation flowed for all of humanity.
(Pope Francis, 9 June 2013)

Anger

Sometimes we're unable to express compassion because, whenever reminded of a particular experience, a hidden reservoir is breached and we're overwhelmed by anger. It may concern how we felt at the abuse we or a loved one suffered, or an injustice experienced which we still carry. That's the sort of thing to take to spiritual direction because, if not, it can have a corrosive effect on us and our relationships while we remain blind to the primary cause. Yet it takes less energy to love and forgive than to stay angry or hold a grudge. Mercy and forgiveness bring peace; each day we need to forgive those who sin against us, not just for their benefit but for ours ... remember, Jesus taught us to daily ask our Father to 'forgive us our trespasses *as we forgive those who trespass against us* ...' (and it would be instructive to ponder why he said 'us' and 'our' rather than 'me' and 'mine').

We know that Jesus occasionally expressed anger – for example, when he encountered the damage caused to some through the abusive way others interpreted the Torah. Anger can also be a consequence of compassion leading Jesus to break the Sabbath Law and, down the ages, his witness has led many to do great things. St Francis saw the destitute and lepers in Assisi but his response wasn't anger, it was loving compassion leading him to reject his aspirational, middle-class upbringing as he sought to respond to the hidden presence of Christ. More recently Fr Bill Kirkpatrick (1927–2018), inspired by Ss Francis of Assisi and Charles of Jesus (de Foucauld, 1858–1916), became a priest of divine compassion for young male prostitutes in London and for victims of HIV/AIDS as he lived a vocation of 'being there' and 'Reaching Out' from Jesus' Heart, which was displayed on the door of his basement oratory.

Blame and mercy

It's through the lens of this Heart that God regards us, as Julian of Norwich said, 'with pity not with blame'. Although being fully human requires living with those (demanding) virtues of compassion and mercy I may look at someone and be more conscious of a little demon passionately whispering in my ear: 'But they're not as good/holy/generous/gifted as *you*!' I might *want* to be compassionate but sin warps my view; rather than being generous, my insecurity, pride, envy, fear that I'll be overlooked or seen as having less value gets in the way – if they're bad I must be better ... *Miserere mei*!

Isaac the Syrian said that if we wish to 'commune with God' we need to 'Strive to be merciful ... A man should first of all begin to be merciful in the measure that our heavenly Father is merciful.' Mercy is an aspect of God and so a virtue that reveals our God-likeness; but if we haven't experienced it, mercy can be difficult to offer as Jesus pointed in the Parable of the Two Sons when the elder became jealous of his father's compassion for the younger. Shame and guilt can also block the development of mercy. So, as *The Cloud of Unknowing* points out: 'If memories of your past actions keep coming between you and God, or any new thought or sinful impulse, you are resolutely to step over them because of your deep love for God. Try to cover them with the "thick cloud of forgetting". And if it is really hard work you can use every dodge, scheme and spiritual stratagem you can find to put them away. Do everything you can to act as if you did not know that these thoughts were strongly pushing in between you and God. Try to look over their shoulders, seeking something else – which is God, shrouded in the cloud of unknowing' (Ch. 31).

The cost of compassionate living

Rejoicing in the graceful light and joy associated with the incarnation and resurrection of the Word made flesh some Christians can feel uncomfortable about the darkness of loss and death, which may be why many (Anglican) Good Friday liturgies are less well attended than those of Easter Day. Yet the heart of our faith embraces both: life comes at a cost, justice and peace are demanding and the struggle with the powers of darkness is painful. Though evil continues to cause suffering and new martyrs will appear until the end of time, our faith tells us that Satan can never win the final battle – we need to be rooted in Christ the Victor.

Yet although the psalmist affirms, 'The LORD is gracious and full of compassion, slow to anger and of great kindness' (145.8), this can be difficult to express. Most agree that it's important to be compassionate and might even consider the virtue commendable but, like many valuable things, it can seem too costly. But because they're aspects of God's nature, fixing the heart on God and nurturing them will also aid our sanctification – even our failures can help if we learn those lessons taught by humility. Devotion to the Sacred Heart doesn't just call us to worship, it opens us to the fullness of divine life until we can say, 'I want my heart, my life, to be like his!' That's what makes the saints so attractive: their lives reveal something of God's radiant beauty.

By its very nature, compassion involves a certain vulnerability. If I felt nothing this virtue would be impossible to express, yet, if I do, I become open to another just as Jesus' own vulnerability led to his suffering, death – and resurrection. Although compassion to that extent is rare there are examples: the story of how the Polish Franciscan priest St Maximilian Kolbe OFM took the place of a young father being sent to a gas chamber in Auschwitz in 1941 is a striking account of how our faith doesn't just call us to be kind but presents us with the uncomfortable fact that it concerns a God who lived by the way of suffering love. Jesus challenges us in simple ways: 'Those who say, "I love God", and hate their brothers or sisters, are liars; for those who do not love a brother or sister whom they have seen, cannot love God whom they have not seen' (1 John 4.20). The compassion of his Heart trumps any sentimentality with which it's associated.

An elder was once asked, 'What is a compassionate heart?' He replied: 'It is a heart on fire for the whole of creation, for humanity, for the birds, for the animals, for demons and all that exists. At the recollection and at the sight of them such a person's eyes overflow with tears owing to the vehemence of the compassion which grips his heart; as a result of his deep mercy his heart shrinks and cannot bear to hear or look on any injury or the slightest suffering of anything in creation. (St Isaac of Syria, Homily 81)

Reflections

How does your faith help you address feelings associated with suffering and desolation?

- What virtues – human qualities – does a Christian need to nurture and why are they difficult?
- What are the differences of allowing our views on social issues to be formed by Christ rather than politicians?
- How might you/your church be called to express divine compassion?

A PRACTICE TO DEVELOP COMPASSION

At the heart of Jesus' teachings is the desire for the well-being of all, the overcoming of divisions and developing an open and inclusive heart. Drawing on a Buddhist 'Loving-kindness' (Metta Bhavana) practice, the following can assist nurturing compassion for ourselves and others and aid growth in the likeness of Christ. This meditation focuses on self, those who have been kind to us, those we feel neutral about and those we dislike. Find a comfortable place to sit.

Introduction

Come, Holy Spirit ✠ and fill my heart with your merciful, Divine Wisdom. Amen.

Place a hand on your heart and formulate your desires into four phrases such as:
May I be filled with your love, O Lord … May your love enfold me.
May *(your partner or close friend)* be filled with your love, O Lord … May your love enfold him/her.
May my friends *(name them)* be filled with your love, O Lord … May your love enfold them.
May *(someone you dislike)* be filled with your love, O Lord … May your love enfold him/her.
These things I ask in the name of Jesus' Compassionate Heart. Amen.

NB.1: Any of these intentions can be used throughout the day, especially when we become conscious of negative feelings towards others. When this happens, another simple practice involves directing these intentions at them:

'May you be well ... may you be happy ... may you know the compassion of Christ.'

NB.2: Practice makes perfect – we can't expect something to grow unless it's tended. As a side benefit, Metta practice can help us experience life in a more positive way.

Merciful God,
may the Compassion of Jesus flow in me / us.
May I / we love all people and the whole of creation
with his compassionate Heart.
May I / we live with Jesus' compassion for all beings.
Amen.

7

The Heart of the Eucharist

'Were not our hearts burning within us while he was talking to us?' ... how he had been made known to them in the breaking of the bread ... (Luke 24.32, 35)

Some years ago my partner and I spent a weekend in Paris. On our first evening we climbed up through the lively district of Montmartre to the great Basilica of Sacré Coeur crowning the hill. Founded in 1875 as the culmination of a long-standing desire to dedicate France to the Sacred Heart, people still flock there to pray throughout the day and night. Here, in the centre of a city pulsing with life, a church is open inviting people to encounter this Heart – and I recalled how, on another evening, two disciples spoke of their hearts being set ablaze as they knew Jesus in the breaking of bread. Into this sacred space people entered with a certain reverence, yet, despite the crowds, there was a homeliness, a prayerfulness, which neither my Methodist upbringing nor Anglican formation prepared me for, even though I'd sung:

> *Jesus, who gave Himself for you*
> *Upon the Cross to die,*
> *Opens to you His Sacred Heart;*
> *Oh, to that Heart draw nigh.*
> *(Edward Caswell, 1814–78)*

As we entered, my attention was attracted by the magnetic white brilliance of the Blessed Sacrament set in a great monstrance (receptacle) raised above the High Altar. The fragile intensity of the Sacrament drew my eyes further, up to the vast mosaic of Christ filling the centre of the apse, his arms open wide and his Heart blazing with golden light as he gazes on the world. Here was a place declaring one thing: God's compassionate love for all – the good, the bad and the indifferent – and I was drawn to kneel and adore. This is the universal and eternal message of the Sacred Heart with its invitation to be silent, still and aware that the world is filled with divine Love.

Although I had only schoolboy French, once the 8pm Mass began, the liturgy was familiar and I became conscious of the power of the priest's invitation, *'Élevons notre cœur'* ('Lift up your hearts'). Mine was moved and enlightened in responding: *'Nous le tournons vers le Seigneur'* ('We lift them to the Lord'); we were being invited to make ourselves present to that Heart above us, an encounter that continues to inspire and inform me no matter how neglectful I am at times.

Christ's eucharistic Heart

The Blessed Sacrament of Holy Communion is Jesus' priceless gift of love. Only the Host is reserved because his Body and Blood are inseparable – his Body animated by his Blood. His presence whenever two or three are gathered together in earthly time (*chronos*) reflects his presence in eternity (*kairos*) which, through the power of the Holy Spirit, is revealed in every eucharistic celebration, yet a Presence that is with us wherever the Sacrament is reserved. The Eucharist can never be just a recollection of the Last Supper, but is a living memorial of the Passover and celebration of the eternal Supper of the Lamb (hence we join the angels in their song – Revelations 5.8f.) revealing and inviting us into the very Heart of God.

There is, then, a strong connection between the Eucharist and the Sacred Heart – even their feasts are conjoined: the latter's on the day (Friday) after the Octave of Corpus Christi which falls on the Thursday following Trinity Sunday. Being a Friday the Feast of the Sacred Heart is a reminder of the connection between the physicality of Christ's gift of himself on the cross and in the Eucharist, each informed by the love of the Heart that animated his offering. This connection is made clear by the Preface (the variable thanksgiving at the beginning of the Eucharistic Prayer) of the Sacred Heart:

> *... raised up high on the Cross,*
> *(Jesus) gave himself up for us with a wonderful love*
> *and poured out blood and water from his pierced side,*
> *the wellspring of the Church's Sacraments,*
> *so that, won over to the open heart of the Saviour,*
> *all might draw water joyfully from the springs of salvation.*

This is reflected in George Herbert's poem 'The Agonie': 'Love is that liquor sweet and most divine / Which my God feels as blood and I as wine', words alerting us to the way the 'liquor' of love is pumped through Christ's body by the action of his Heart. It is this blood that, together with water – sources of Baptism and the Eucharist – flowed from Jesus' side on being pierced by the Holy Lance. Witnessed by his Mother and the beloved disciple here is the ultimate, eternal image of his love by which we're reborn and renewed.

This is my body ... my blood

This gift is constantly affirmed in John 6 which, because the Gospel offers no account of the Last Supper, is considered his great eucharistic discourse (especially vv.22–end). 'I am the living bread that came down from heaven ...', John records Jesus saying, '... my flesh is true food and my blood is true drink. Those who eat my flesh and drink my blood abide in me, and I in them ...', something so shocking then as now that many of his disciples 'no longer went about with him' (John 6.66).

This Gospel is considered by some to be a mystical work – it doesn't offer a record of events but an exposition of the hidden, inner life of Christ; so while John wants us to reflect on the way Jesus is truly present in the Sacrament he makes it clear that 'feeding' on him doesn't make us cannibals – 'It is the spirit that gives life; the flesh is useless' (6.63). John holds the balance between the truth of 'this is my body' and what is to be discerned *through* that body; for in the Blessed Sacrament we receive the *Heart* of who Jesus is; it is that which gives life. The physicality of our incarnational faith prevents it being viewed in a purely 'spiritual' way, yet we need to see beneath externals to the heart of what they communicate.

We know Margaret-Mary felt herself 'penetrated' by Christ when she was praying before the Blessed Sacrament, and Francis de Sales, in his *Introduction to the Devout Life*, advises us to receive the gift of Holy Communion frequently because the Lord became our food in order to 'penetrate' us with Love and unite us with his Heart. This is reflected in that simple but profound prayer offered by the priest at the Eucharist as a little water is poured into the wine during the Preparation of the Gifts: 'By the mystery of this water and wine may we come to share in the divinity of Christ who humbled himself to share in our humanity.' The Heart of the Sacrament needs to speak into ours and stir desire for what is conveyed, something aided by genuflecting or profoundly bowing to the sacramental Presence; we are to 'lower' our heart before his in an act of loving adoration and thankfulness. Raising hands in prayer can also help lift our hearts, enabling them to express the depths of our joy, wonder and desire.

I have found this Heart in the Eucharist when I have found there the Heart of my Sovereign, of my Friend, of my Brother, that is to say, the Heart of my friend and Redeemer … Come, my brethren, let us enter into this amiable Heart never again to go out from It. (Bernard of Clairvaux, Vitis Mystica, Ch. III)

A eucharistic Heart

As the word 'Eucharist' is Greek for thanksgiving, Jesus' Heart is a thankful Heart. Thankfulness enlightens the heart, delivering it from the darkness of hatred and nurturing its growth in the image of Christ's; thankfulness has the power to cleanse the heart's caverns, bringing light into the darkness and, as a precursor of joy, setting it free.

In the Orthodox liturgy the priest, preparing for the Eucharistic Prayer, first says: 'Let us stand aright! Let us stand with fear! Let us attend! That we may offer the Holy Oblation in peace.' I first experienced standing around the altar for the Eucharistic Prayer in 1966 on visiting the Society of the Sacred Mission at their theological college at Kelham, Nottinghamshire. Having to leave the comfortable security of 'my' seat and feeling somewhat exposed as I stood with 70 others circling the altar I came to realize how this expresses what is said before the Peace in the Anglican liturgy: 'We are the body of Christ.' We're not just a gathering of individuals but a body whose focus is to be Christ's beating Heart present in our midst on the altar. Here is the 'centre around which life revolves and the heart of our prayer life' (Society of St Francis, *Principles*, Day 15). We stand with wondering love, knowing we're to shift awareness from attending to the word of scripture to the Word made flesh. The invitation we're given isn't to 'lift up your minds' or 'remember Christ is with us', but to raise the *heart* to God's Heart. It's a Mystery the bodily eye cannot see, but 'faith, our outward sense befriending, makes our inward vision clear', for we stand with the holy ones in the divine Presence. This is what must move our heart; for we arn't merely 'attending a service' but part of a worshipping, mystical body:

> ... *if you have been raised with Christ, seek the things that are above, where Christ is, seated at the right hand of God. Set your minds on things that are above, not on things that are on earth, for you have died, and your life is hidden with Christ in God. (Colossians 3.1–3)*

We stand with joy and wonder as those who would welcome a special guest into their home or, as Psalm 24.7 recalls:

> *Lift up your hearts, O gates!*
> *and be lifted up, O ancient doors!*
> *that the King of glory may come in.*

That psalm, sung in the Jerusalem Temple, is associated both with Advent as we await the coming of our King and the Ascension when we celebrate Jesus' entrance into the New Jerusalem. It's also a reflection of Lamentations 3.41: 'Let us lift up our hearts as well as our hands to God in heaven', at which point, when heart and Heart are as one, we are to 'Rejoice in the Lord always ...' That's the cry of angels and mortals, a response aided by the will not least because, at times, the will needs to nudge a distracted or sleepy heart. This is the time when, standing with the saints before the transformative Mystery, we encounter the foreshadowing of God's ultimate desire for creation.

Preparing the heart

It was Jesus' heartfelt desire to share this Passover with his disciples and it was that same desire that moved him to promise to remain with them, a promise fulfilled through this sacrament, for 'Whoever eats of this bread will live for ever; and the bread that I will give for the life of the world is my flesh' (John 6.51). This is the one, eternal, defining gift of fiery love uniting Lover and beloved and, sharing in it, we need to give ourselves totally to him as he gives himself to us – body, mind and spirit.

Priest and congregation affirm common-union with our great High Priest, our hearts desiring to be at one with his. We need to be present in a recollected way, attentive to what is happening so we can know the love of his Heart for us, *now*. This transformation of the gifts on the altar by the Spirit's breath is an affirmation that creation is to be liberated as we long for that exchange of hearts which is the meaning of Holy Communion. We become part of his life who would transform our heart into his 'burning furnace of charity', as the Litany of the Sacred Heart says ... does that thought inflame you?

And because Jesus enlivens the hearts of those hungry to receive him the importance of preparing for this by prayer, penitence and (if physically able) an hour's fasting has long been recognized. Reflecting on the Gospel of the day and quietly praying in church (rather than talking to friends) before the celebration are beneficial means for the heart to welcome its Maker.

The Blessed Sacrament of Love

Every eucharistic celebration is another Christmas, the Incarnation of Love. Love was seen, clothed in flesh, suffered, died, entered hell, rose from the grave and ascended into heaven's glory. And although mortal eyes no longer behold Jesus in the crib, the eye of our heart can see the wonder of Emmanuel – the Love of God with us – in this sacrament. Beneath these gifts of creation lies the means of opening our heart to the power of Christ's limitless love, a love that doesn't depend on our worthiness.

> *O OCEAN of love,*
> *stillness profound,*
> *light and life of all who come to thee,*
> *draw me into thy still peace,*
> *that all the noise of things be stilled*
> *and the music of my soul be all one harmony,*
> *thyself alone, my GOD,*
> *my all.*
> (*Gilbert Shaw*, A Pilgrim's Book of Prayers*)*

St Claude de la Colombière confirmed that the presence of the 'ocean of mercy' in the Heart of Jesus is also present in the Eucharist for both reveal, in the words of Julian of Norwich, that 'love was his meaning: Who reveals it to you? Love. What did he reveal to you? Love. Why does he reveal it to you? For Love' (*Revelations*, Ch. 86). We're made by Love for love – the one is to reflect the Other.

Charles of Jesus, the great martyr for Christ in North Africa, had a profound love for the Heart of the Blessed Sacrament. He built a small hermitage at Beni Abbes, an oasis on the Algeria–Morocco border, for the 'Fraternity of the Sacred Heart of Jesus', where he sought to live a radical Christian inclusivity. In one letter he wrote, 'I want all the inhabitants, be they Christian, Muslim or Jewish, to look on me as their brother, the universal brother', a desire born of his devotion to Christ's universal Heart emblazoned on his habit:

God has created us so that we all be brothers on earth
as the angels are brothers in heaven;
God wants us to love him above all things.
He wants us to love people as we love ourselves;
This heart written on my robe is to remind me of God
    and people
in order to love them.
(Some of the first phrases he learnt in Arabic)

He realized the value of spending time each day in silent prayer before the Most Holy Sacrament and, although many of us cannot, the practice offered in some churches of a Holy Hour when it is exposed in a monstrance for the prayer of silent adoration is of immense value. At about the same time as St Charles, Andrew SDC wrote his poem 'Sacre Couer', revealing his own devotion to the compassionate, eucharistic Heart of Jesus:

> *Dear Heart, Who in Thy tender love didst come*
> *Not from some cavernous and vast womb*
> *Of cold and passionless eternity,*
> *But didst in human wise take flesh for me*
> *Of sweet St Mary's fair virginity,*
> *and made 'midst men Thy home,*
>
> *Help me to see the greatest in the least,*
> *The whole of life is one great Eucharist;*
> *in common ways and simple loyalties*
> *To find hid treasure of high sanctities,*
> *as Love links symbols to realities*
> *in Thy blest altar Feast.*
> *(Andrew SDC, *Prayers from Father Andrew*)*

BEHOLD, THE HEART OF LOVE

Devotion to the Sacred Heart has a twofold object: it honours first with adoration and public worship the Heart of flesh of Jesus Christ, and secondly the infinite love with which this Heart has burned for us since its creation, and with which it is still consumed in the Sacrament of our altars. (St Peter Julian Eymard, 1811–68, A Reflection on Corpus Christi*)*

Peoples' hearts can be warmed by someone's compassionate gaze and we come before the gaze of Jesus' Heart whenever the Sacrament is exposed for contemplation. We can be present to him who is present to us and practice that silent prayer of longing love: Jesus, I adore you …! The deepest part of God's being burns with love for each of us and we, in turn, are to be ablaze with love for him as we seek to love our sisters and brothers – and our very selves – in obedience to his word. Our churches need to be places where people can come and adore him who longed – and longs – to be with us; where we can talk with him or just rest with him and know that he is fully present to us; where we can curl up before him who opens his Heart to us in this Blessed Sacrament of Divine Compassion.

One of the simplest devotions we can practise is to come to Jesus in this way and 'be there' with him who is in all places and fills all things, yet truly present before us in a fragment of bread. It's a Presence requiring no speech, the only effort being to attend to him and him alone. Might it be possible for churches to offer this contemplative practice – maybe for an hour each month – even if few come? It's even possible to buy and install a tabernacle with a transparent glass screen behind which the Sacrament is exposed for our loving prayer and adoration, blessing all who come into his Presence. What a wonderful means of renewing and refreshing the spiritual life this offers, for the Sacred Heart of the Eucharist is the doorway into Christ.

But even if we cannot find a church where the brilliance of the Host shines out we can always take him with us in the 'monstrance of our heart', as Francis of Assisi recommends: 'We should make a dwelling-place within ourselves where He can stay, He who is the Lord God Almighty, Father, Son and Holy Spirit' (*The Rule and the Life of the Brothers and Sisters of the Third Order*, Ch. 2, 8).

> *O wonderful loftiness and stupendous dignity! O sublime humility! O humble sublimity! The Lord of the universe, God and the Son of God, so humbles Himself that for our salvation He hides Himself under an ordinary piece of bread! Brothers, look at the humility of God, and pour out your hearts before Him! Humble yourselves that you may be exalted by Him! Hold back nothing of yourselves for yourselves, that He Who gives Himself totally to you may receive you totally!*
> *(Francis of Assisi, Letter to the Entire Order, 1225–26)*

Reflections

- Why is it important to recall the Real Presence of the Heart of Jesus in the Blessed Sacrament and what might help you express love for and devotion to Christ there?
- Knowing that the Heart of Jesus is an 'ocean of love', what might you/your church do to reflect that?
- 'Father, I abandon myself into your hands.' What feelings do you notice when praying that and how might Jesus respond?

Spiritual exercises

- On going to a eucharistic celebration direct your heart's attention to the Gifts to be received and reflect on the wonder of God's coming to you, beneath the sacramental form of bread and wine, as he came to Mary and Joseph in Bethlehem (meaning 'House of bread').
- Because we are not worthy to come under the roof of God's house or to even gather crumbs fallen from God's table, use this traditional prayer before receiving the Sacrament: 'Lord, I am not worthy that you should enter under my roof, but only say the word, and my soul shall be healed.'
- Find an open church where the Blessed Sacrament is reserved and, in its presence, recall that Jesus is really present, bend your knee and heart before him and spend time in the prayer of loving adoration. Memorize this other prayer of Francis of Assisi:

We adore you, most holy Lord Jesus Christ,
here and in all your churches throughout the world,
and we bless you, because by your Holy Cross
you have redeemed the world.

A PRAYER PRACTICE

Some time (30 minutes?) before the main Sunday (or a week-day) Eucharist, arrange for the Most Holy Sacrament to be placed on the altar (this doesn't require a priest) and publicly pray the Litany of the Sacred Heart (Appendix 4), Rosary, Jesus Prayer, etc. Afterwards keep silence until an appropriate time and replace the Sacrament before the liturgy begins.

Youth meditation

This exercise draws on the appeal to many young people of fantasy films and TV series. The focus is a table covered in coloured cloths and candles around which are cushions, prayer stools and chairs. Songs like 'Jesus, we adore you', 'Ubi caritas' and 'Be still, for the presence of the Lord' could be sung throughout.

Talk about 'seeing' and how some important things, like love, aren't visible. Read from *The Little Prince*: 'It is only with the heart that one can see rightly; *what is essential is invisible to the eye'*; explain the concept of the 'heart', 'sacramental-seeing' and the use of 'heart meditation'. Place a monstrance containing the Blessed Sacrament in the centre surrounded by tealights – maybe burn incense in a bowl before it. Lead a relaxation and centring exercise using the Host as the focus and offer a meditation on (e.g.) John 15.1–4, inviting people to imagine Jesus' Heart enfolding theirs. Ask if there's anything they want to silently say to Jesus present in the Sacrament … Conclude with meditative music (and Benediction in silence).

8

The Cosmic Heart

The little space within the heart is as great as this vast universe. The heavens and the earth are there, and the sun, and the moon, and the stars; fire and lightning and winds are there; and all that now is and all that is not: for the whole universe is in Him and He dwells within our heart. (Swami Krishnananda, The Chandogya Upanishad, Ch. 4, Sec. 1)

Long ago, in the days of my childhood, my mother would take me cycling from the suburb's edge where we lived to the small village in which she had grown up in Edwardian England. My memories are of delight as we gently pedalled through narrow, winding country lanes whose lush grassy banks, in late springtime, were full of the tiny, delicate, white flowers of cow-parsley before plunging into shady green tunnels made by the branches of overhanging trees. Eventually we arrived at the village green with its large, ornate, circular Victorian water pump and scattering of houses, shops and pubs before heading to the Norman church to tend the grave of her childhood friend and eat a picnic lunch.

The 'anima mundi'

Most of us can trace our ancestry back to an agricultural world. Our forebears interacted with the countryside in ways we can hardly imagine and part of its appeal might be that our roots recall that lost world from which we came, something William Wordsworth (1770–1850) expressed in his 'Ode on Intimations of Immortality':

> *Our birth is but a sleep and a forgetting;*
> *The Soul that rises with us, our life's Star,*
> *Hath had elsewhere its setting*
> *And cometh from afar;*
> *Not in entire forgetfulness,*
> *And not in utter nakedness,*
> *But trailing clouds of glory do we come*
> *From God, who is our home ...*

This may be one reason why we're drawn to spend time in places where the soul can be refreshed by the song of birds and the sight and smell of trees and cut-grass, where it's easy to encounter the world's 'soul' (*anima mundi*), the Christ, who holds all creation in being.

Godly encounters

The Creator's Heart is the source of all that is life-giving. Today many are again conscious of the need to reverence our sustaining Mother Earth; for all the internet offers it can't answer our deepest needs but can prevent us penetrating further than what appears on the screen before our eyes. Yet do we always recognize and give thanks for nature; for rain as well as sunshine, for wind, fire, soil and all Earth's other gifts? We know the world wasn't created in seven days, but only faith can help us realize that nature hides a Divine presence – it's not just there for us to use and abuse. How far are we prepared to reverence creation and share Earth's fruits equally, or do we want to hoard them for ourselves? Looking upon nature we need to recognize and give thanks for its beauty and realize its goodness, a goodness that delights the heart of the Creator (Genesis 1.31). Even gardens, when not paved over or covered by plastic grass, can reveal Divine wonder in bush and flower and refresh us when we plunge bare hands into humus, our skin encountering it's Mother.

Within Orthodoxy there's a wonderful practice recalling this sacred 'atoneness' – when praying before an icon (or at other times) the sign of the cross is made with trinitarian thumb and the first two fingertips joined, the fourth bent into contact with the palm symbolizing Christ's incarnation. The forehead is touched before, bending profoundly, those same fingers touch the ground (on which we walk and in which we may be buried) and concluding by marking the shoulders from left to right tracing the horizon of earth, sea and sky. Naming the Source of all life (Father/Creator), he who came to make all things whole (Son) and the (Holy) Spirit who constantly – invisibly – moves through creation to bring it to glory, these faith-filled actions affirm that, while we're of earth, we're destined for glory.

CREATION'S HEART

The great secret, the great mystery, is this:
there is a heart of the world ...
and this heart is the heart of Christ.
(Pierre Teilhard de Chardin SJ, unpublished Journal 6)

Although my faith-journey began with the concept of a God 'out there', something shifted when I discovered Catholicism's materiality and began to relish an incarnational, sacramental way of seeing. God is as much 'in' here as 'out' there; and to follow Jesus involves the worship of an *in*-mattered God.

St Angela of Foligno (1248–1309), a Franciscan Tertiary, expressed this as she saw the Host being elevated at Mass:

> *The eyes of my soul were immediately opened. In a vision I saw the fullness of God in which I could see and comprehend the whole of creation ... And in all that I saw, I could perceive nothing except the presence of the power of God, in a way totally indescribable. And my soul, in an excess of wonder, cried out: 'The world is pregnant with God!' And I embraced the whole of creation like a small object – what is on this side and what is beyond the sea, the abyss, the sea itself, and everything else – but the power of God overflowed and filled everything ... He then said: 'Behold now my humility.' I was given an insight into the deep humility of God towards man. By comprehending such an unspeakable power and by seeing such a deep humility, my soul was completely astonished, and esteemed itself to be nothing at all. (Memorial, Ch. 6)*

'The world is pregnant with God!' reflected Angela's contemporary, Julian of Norwich, who saw the whole of creation in a hazelnut and heard God say: 'It is all that is made.' Marvelling at how it existed Julian sensed God adding: 'It lasts and ever will, because God loves it.' To be human, then, is to be part of that beloved whole which is in those 'birth pangs' noted by Paul (Romans 8.18–25); this means that *life* inevitably involves the mystery of pain, anguish and grief as well as wonder, joy and happiness.

Western culture has long overlooked – denied – the Divine heart of creation, treating nature as a commodity to be used (and abused) according to *our* will ... although we're now beginning to recognize the consequence of soul-less materialism promoting the gods of financial profitability, celebrity and glamour. But the more attention we give to things offered for our enjoyment or as the goal of our desires the harder it is to know that the wonder of life involves both the immediately appealing *and* that which might initially repel. External temptations, along with all the 'drugs' we consume, can numb us and may need resisting lest we're misled and fail to realize the true cost of living. Our Spirit-inbreathed, incarnational faith says: 'we know that we're flesh and blood but to be fully human means recognizing and responding to the Spirit who gives life', the divine 'glue' making all whole.

Sacraments of creation

 When bread and wine are taken, offered and the Spirit – who enables creation – invoked upon them, the hidden yeast of Christ is activated for these gifts to become his Body and Blood. We cannot see this Mystery (any more than we can normally see the body's heart nor 'prove' the existence of Love), but the notion that the cosmos is merely heartless, chaotic or meaningless doesn't quite tally with most people's experience. However, rather than trying to understand this Mystery perhaps we're meant to 'stand under' it with a contemplative gaze, for God 'is not so much the object of our knowledge as the cause of our wonder' (Kallistos Ware, *The Orthodox Way*, p. 16). In contemplating this Mystery the reflective person will notice its effect on the heart and might even realize that being fully present to it has a cleansing, wholesome effect satisfying the heart while enabling us to feel at-one with the Spirit's pulse.

> *It is not within our power to understand the universe,*
> *whose centre and circumference are God.*
> *(Cardinal Nicholas of Cusa, 1401–64,*
> De Docta Ignorantia*)*

Saints like Cuthbert of Lindisfarne, Francis of Assisi and Seraphim of Sarov realized this, enabling them to speak to birds, play with fish and know that everything is co-related: Brother Sun, Sister Moon, Mother Earth ... We are not just 'stewards' of creation, we're *one with all that is*. 'Blessed are you, Lord, God of all creation ...' Earth needs us to be her priests, ordained or not, offering our sacrifice of thanks and praise as we go about daily life. We need to beware the dangers offered by 'virtual' life separating us from created reality ... can human flourishing *really* be achieved by our ability to own the latest expensive smart devices or piece of consumer AI equipment which, by its very nature, *is* artificial and not a creation of the Sacred Heart? Or are the purveyors of such technology encouraging an addiction that will rob us of the means to connect us with *real* life ...?

THE SACRED HEART OF THE UNIVERSE

Under the symbol of the Sacred Heart the divine assumed for me, the form of fire ... (T)hrough its power to become universal this fire proved able to invade and impregnate with love the whole atmosphere of the world in which I lived ... It is in the Sacred Heart that the conjunction of the divine and the cosmic has taken place ... There lies the power that from the beginning has attracted and conquered me ... All the later development of my interior life has been nothing other than the evolution of that seed. (de Chardin, The Heart of Matter, *p. 43)*

Angela of Foligno's sense of 'unspeakable power' and 'deep humility' illustrates the paradox at the heart of faith which challenges anyone satisfied with a prayer life that merely 'seems OK ...', forgetting Christ's invitation to enter the depths of relationship with him. Teilhard plunged into those depths expressing the wonder he encountered in an essay entitled *Le Milieu Divin*; he saw the Sacred Heart coinciding with the heart of the universe, calling this the 'Omega Point' as Christ lovingly reconciles all things to himself (Colossians 1.20), opening devotion to this Heart beyond any particular anatomical portrayals. It is the source of that Love which, if it flows in and through us, can help the world's healing and bring us to the fullness of our humanity.

He found that those words in the Eucharistic Prayer, 'This is my body', reach beyond a small piece of bread bringing the entire mystical body of Christ into being to enable its completion. He saw that

> *the true Host ... is the universe which is continually being more intimately penetrated and vivified by Christ. From the most distant origin of things until their unforeseeable consummation, through the countless convulsions of boundless space, the whole of nature is slowly and irresistibly undergoing the supreme consecration. Fundamentally – since all time and for ever – one single thing is being made in creation: the body of Christ. (de Chardin, Mon Universe, p. 65)*

Secularized humanity is blind to this notion of cosmic sacredness, yet the eye of artists, poets and contemplatives directs us to take that long, loving look enabling us to see into the world's 'heart', something Elizabeth Barratt Browning (1806–61) realized in an allusion to Moses and the burning bush:

> *Earth's crammed with heaven,*
> *And every common bush afire with God,*
> *But only he who sees takes off his shoes;*
> *The rest sit round and pluck blackberries.*
> *(Elizabeth Barrett Browning, 1806–61, Aurora Leigh)*

Recognizing Christ at the centre of all matter Teilhard wrote of a 'Christified universe', a universe eucharistically transfigured by the One who consecrates all matter to reveal divinity (Romans 8.19, Revelation 13.8). He recounts the story of a 'friend' who, during the First World War, entered a French church near the Front: sitting before a picture of the Sacred Heart he found it gradually 'melted' as the light coming from it seemed to reach into the 'furthest sphere of Matter' causing the Universe to vibrate (*The Heart of Matter*, p. 64). He saw the 'incommunicable beauty of Christ' shining in everything, revealing itself as both personal Love and cosmic Power and drawing him to worship. This is what Thomas Merton OCSO (1915–68) experienced when in Louisville 'at the corner of Fourth and Walnut' he saw each person's face 'shining like the sun' (*Conjectures of a Guilty Bystander*).

> *'Throughout my life, by means of my life,*
> *the world has little by little caught fire in my sight until,*
> *aflame all around me, it has become almost luminous*
> *from within ...*
> *(de Chardin,* Le Milieu Divin, *p. 14)*

Some think this must be pantheism – all things are God; that viewing a beautiful sunset, magnificent seascape or majestic mountains will simply mesmerize us, leading to a form of idolatry. Yet I recall how on clear dark Dorset nights, after leaving Compline in the chapel at Hilfield Friary, I would sometimes walk to a meadow where my eyes would be drawn up into the star-studded band of the Milky Way stretching from one end of the heavens to the other and my heart would be moved to worship the Creator. I'd have a sense of connectedness with the heart of the universe, of being at one with Mother Earth and our Sisters and Brothers, the Stars and Planets, who illuminate the night. It reminded me of the importance of looking to the Mystery expressed by creation, that work of God's hands, and realize the Sacred *in* all things (pan-*en*-theism), for the heartbeat of God pulses through the universe. Providing our heart is awake to their inner being that being can, like a magnet, draw us until we finally respond: 'the heavens declare the glory of God' (Psalm 19.1).

Gazing on the heart of this 'other' I've found myself profoundly moved out of my 'self', free to respond with a 'yes!' to God. From simple leaf, tiny insect or fragile butterfly to the celestial panoply my heart is drawn into desiring at-oneness and I notice my own sense of humanity being nourished and affirmed. I am more 'me' as I am embraced by this Other, leading St Bonaventure to consider the universe as a 'ladder' for ascending to God (cf. Bonaventure's, *The Soul's Journey into God*).

Cosmic communion

Francis of Assisi knew this universal oneness – interconnectedness – was the expression of Love, that profound Trinitarian mystery that attracts us and longs for our response and is realized through the individual and cosmic Sacred Heart. Though its representations can be gaudy, touching, naïve, emotional or sentimental we're invited into the Heart of God resonating with the world's pain as well as its brilliance; here is the Heart of life. This is not a vague 'spiritual' experience, but is an encounter with God-in-all-things, which is why matter matters and Heart speaks to heart. Teilhard saw Christ's 'amorized' Heart – a heart fired by love – penetrating and enlivening creation, calling it the 'motor of evolution', the source of Creative Love afire with energy enabling development and growth. He believed surrender to communion with evolution's God was the way to the point where the 'Heart of the universalized Christ' coincided 'with the heart of amorized Matter', before which Mystery he could only worship (de Chardin, *The Heart of Matter*, pp. 43–9).

Thomas Merton developed these thoughts through his short but powerful meditation *La Pointe Vierge* (the 'Virgin Point'). It tells of the way there is, in the very centre of our being, a 'point of nothingness' which is the 'pure glory of God in us' as incorrupt as a flawless diamond which, because it is in all of us, would blaze like the sun should all the facets of light come together.

> *Lord, I was made for Thee,*
> *So let me rest*
> *Not otherwise than on Thy breast.*
> *Let the pure thought of Thee*
> *Quiet my mind,*
> *In Thy dear Heart my heart*
> *Its haven find.*
> *Yea, let myself, this little soul,*
> *Come to so great a goal.*
> *For though of clay Thou madest me,*
> *My clay was touched with Thine eternity,*
> *And I am 'restless till I rest in thee'.*
> *(Andrew SDC, 'Echo of S Augustine')*

Being and belonging

Just as gazing on Mother Earth with love's eye can lead to a sense of connectedness and evoke reverence so can contemplation of the stars, for we're made of the same stuff. And if it doesn't that suggests the heart needs awakening to realize that wonder, love and praise of which it's capable and for which it was made. In this way our sense of belonging can widen from the particular (*my* family, home, nation) to a greater sense of belonging as a creature in creation.

Jesus seemed to recognize this as he reached out ('who is my mother ...) and Paul taught ' ... what matters is a new creation' (Galatians 6.15). Realizing ourselves as this new being whose heart is to be filled with love, compassion and mercy we need to be mindful, 'heart-full', of our calling. Even though we may have a particular love it is Jesus' Sacred Heart that is to enable our loving; gazing on it, ours can be warmed and know an invitation to grow beyond the limits of self, the challenge of renewal ('a new heart create for me, O God ...', Psalm 51.10) and invitation to be refreshed.

THE WELL OF DIVINE ENCOUNTER

'The water that I will give will become in [you]
a spring of water gushing up to eternal life.'
(John 4.14)

Throughout the scriptures there are these signs, symbols and metaphors concerning the Sacred Heart. Though some may be gender-specific they connect with everyone; the simple act of sitting and being open to our inner depths – our generative 'womb' – can be profoundly important in accessing our creativeness both in prayer and life. Our 'waters' may become muddied, our well and cave fill with discarded 'stuff' in the hope such 'stuff' will disappear; we might fear being drowned, but there is Jesus' constant reminder that 'out of the believer's heart shall flow rivers of living water' (John 7.38). Entrance into these life-giving depths involves learning how to still those rivers and avoid getting caught up in the rubbish floating around. And the deeper we go the more we'll discover, for, at heart, water bubbles from God's own Heart-spring.

The story of Jesus' encounter with a woman at a well in John 4 is more than just an account of overcoming cultural taboos (talking with an unknown woman) or religious barriers (Jews vs Samaritans). It becomes apparent that he was concerned with her heart as an image of his and, drawing on Isaiah's prophesy, 'With joy you will draw water from the wells of salvation' (12.3), tells her: 'The water that I will give will become in [you] a spring of water gushing up to eternal life.' Later he adds: 'Let anyone who is thirsty come to me, and let the one who believes in me drink. As the scripture has said, "Out of the believer's heart shall flow rivers of living water"' (John 7.37f.). Jesus knew of her need for those waters-of-life, for he too thirsted, so 'Give *me* a drink' were his first words to her.

Our thirst is a consequence of God's thirst to be in relationship with us: 'Let Christ quench your thirst, for streams of living water flow from his heart' (St Ambrose of Milan, 335–97). That 'divine thirst' is within everyone, yet how many drink from their well? Cheap lager may satisfy for a while, but only 'living water' can answer our profoundest need – and it doesn't come in plastic bottles.

At the Great Easter Vigil we gather at another well, the font, to renew our baptismal promises as we sing: 'Water of Life, cleanse and refresh us; raise us to life in Christ Jesus.' Gazing into this well, into the world's heart, we realize that the further we peer the darker it becomes; yet the freshest water may come from the depths where light can't penetrate. Tempting though it may be to give up the contemplative gaze, or tiring to keep lowering our 'bucket', the invitation comes by way of love – and love will, at times, require a sheer effort of will to stay, lovingly, present to the One present to us.

'Go to the Heart of Jesus and draw from it,
and when you need more,
go back to the Source and draw again.'
(St Madeleine Sophie Barat, 1779–1865,
Foundress of the Society of the Sacred Heart of Jesus)

'Reconcile yourself to wait in the darkness as long as necessary ...', said the author of *The Cloud of Unknowing*, '... go on longing after him who you love' (Ch. 3).

The heart's cave

Caves, which often appear in scripture, offer a womb-like, primal entrance into their heart, their (creative) depths. Elijah sat at the entrance to one and heard the silent word of God; it was not in a shed that Jesus was born but in a cave, a slit, leading into the heart of Mother Earth, and it was in a cave he was buried. Although many books have been written about caves few consider their Christian symbolism and the (Western) churches have overlooked the profound importance of attending to Christ's descent into the underworld in 1 Peter 3.18f., into the mysterious heart of the Earth. Various Desert Elders occupied them, as some still do, and cave-like crypts provide foundations for great churches. The 'cave of the heart' is a metaphor for the place of the soul's indwelling and enlivening where we can listen to the Spirit speaking; to dismiss their value (and that of wells and springs etc.) because that's 'pagan' robs us of access to the gems and minerals hidden there.

Yet while they were also places of imprisonment and burial, this place of lifelessness paradoxically enabled Jesus to visit and set free those held in the 'prison-house' of Hades (Ephesians 4.9–10) as he liberated that deathly place. Is there anything that needs freeing in your heart – 'out of the depths I cry to you, O LORD' (Psalm 130.1)? So it was that the Desert Elder, Abba Moses, advised: 'Go into your cell (cave), your cell (heart) will teach you everything.' Teresa of Avila tells us to keep on searching the caves ('rooms') of our 'Interior Mountain' and realize the beauty of the soul. 'Remember your dignity,' she told her sisters, describing the soul as a diamond – the 'immortal diamond' of one of Gerard Manley

Hopkins' poems. Are we, in turn, aware of the beauty of our soul, the 'wonder of our being' (Psalm 138)?

> *If you possessed the spiritual insight to penetrate the invisible world, the atoms of the visible world would also become unveiled to you, but if you regard these with the eye of the intellect, you will never comprehend love as you should. (Abū Ḥamīd bin Abū Bakr Ibrāhī, 1146–1221, Conference of the Birds)*

It might seem that being aware of our 'inner beauty' suggests an emphasis on 'self', something that can be dangerous as, again paradoxically, it can prevent that growth which depends on moving beyond 'self' and interacting with the world. Self-concern can feed into the belief that we should try to get as much from life as possible, a narrative embraced by some to the extent that they've forgotten that giving is more important than getting. Earlier societies realized themselves as part of the greater whole and understood life as a costly gift for which they needed to give thanks rather than viewing it as a means of self-satisfaction. People recognized they needed to be in communion and one consequence of today's emphasis on individuality is that we can ignore this fundamental need.

The Sacred Heart is personal and cosmic. He who is Son of the Father is also the Word by which creation came into being; both humankind and the cosmos share a sacredness and failure of concern, for one has implications for the other; to act as if nature was there simply to satisfy our demands insults the Creator. Yet for the sake of gaining power some declare we have the right to act as we want regardless of the cost to Mother Earth whose heart cries out in agony. It is part of the creed of those who, as Oscar Wilde said in *The Picture of Dorian Gray*, 'know the price of everything and the value of nothing'; concern for the financial wealth of the few causes others to suffer and runs counter to the gospel of love – love for the whole of creation of which everyone and everything is part. Greatness isn't found through wealth and power but by exercising the virtues.

Whatever the appeal of the Sacred Heart it is not solely a means of pious devotion for it concerns what lies most deeply within that Mystery named God. Although these reflections are coming to an end, the gospel that emanates from the Heart of Jesus continues to speak to every heart, calling us to place the love of God at the centre of our lives and to love and serve whatever God loves. It calls for a constant conversion of our heart through its purification; to abide in this Heart and realize and respond to its presence in the whole cosmos, for as Bonaventure knew:

> *Creation is like a beautiful song that flows in the most excellent of harmonies, but it is a song that God freely desires to sing into the vast spaces of the universe. There's nothing that compels God to chant this hymn of the universe, creation is the sacred outflow of a loving God in whose infinite, dynamic goodness we share. (Sentences, d.44,q,1,a.3, conc.)*

Although we may have ceased to acknowledge the *anima mundi*, privatized the spiritual, dismissed religion and scorned practices and disciplines taught by the mystics, we cannot restore abused nature simply by addressing practical environmental concerns, as important as that is. Instead of being slaves to consumerism, fundamentalist dogmatism and the dictats of demagogues we need to proclaim that the world has a heart, a heart that reflects Christ's and whose meaning is love. At a time when many have lost any notion of either an incarnate God or the divine mystery of their being, our greatest challenge may be to help them realize that the heart's emptiness and deepest desire can only be answered as the creature seeks union with the Creator. Nothing less can, in the end, satisfy. We are to have that same desire for union with our bridegroom as he has for us as the Song of Songs and St John of the Cross so powerfully express.

To be fully human is to be a person whose heart is being formed by *that* gospel, a person who loves the 'Other' beyond all others and realizes all creation is enlivened by the love of *that* Heart – a love that needs expressing in every aspect of life. To be fully human requires our heart to mirror his who told us that fullness of life comes through its purification – individually and universally – and is the way we come to the vision of our Creator.

Reflections

- How might your church give attention to the Sacred Heart in creation? What difference might that make?
- Caves, wells, water – what do they teach us about our faith?
- How could we encourage people to visit the 'cave of the heart'.

Spiritual exercises

- Go outside and take time to allow your senses – sight, hearing, smell, etc. – to encounter creation (earth, wind, heat, etc.); give praise and thanks and, like Francis of Assisi, acknowledge each as brother and sister in your heart.

- Notice Mother Earth's brokenness and recognize the damage we have caused her. Consider that this wound is God's Heart and confess your part in this and consider ways you can be an agent of reconciliation and healing.

A CELEBRATION OF THE SACRED HEART OF CREATION

The following could be incorporated into a Cosmic Eucharist taking the place of the intercessions, or as a 'stand-alone' liturgy. An image of the Sacred Heart and votive lamp stands before the altar. If held indoors objects from nature – earth, water, leaves, plants, candles (light), etc. are placed near where people gather. There are online Propers for a Creation Eucharist with appropriate readings: or Genesis 1.1–13; Revelations 21.1–5; John 1.1–14.

After the Gospel, talk of the way nature bears the imprint of its Maker and that believing in a Creator means believing in a divine origin to all that exists, not that Genesis is to be considered as a 'scientific' work. As with all created things the natural world is an expression of what exists at the very heart of God, meaning all creation is sacred.

Follow this with a short centring exercise – be still, breathe deeply, descend from mind into heart, let go of distractions, etc. Invite people to wander outside for 15 minutes slowly exploring their surroundings, or walk around the 'centrepiece', until their attention is taken by one particular object which, if possible, they should take to their place, sit with and notice how it speaks to their heart. Afterwards invite them into a deeper encounter with their object – looking at, feeling and smelling it while allowing the experience to descend into the heart, recognizing that this is an encounter with something sacred – how does that make them feel? What response might they make? After a suitable period they should place their object before the Sacred Heart as the *Benedicite* (*Song of Azariah / The Three Children*, Daniel 3.57–88) is recited. A Eucharist continues with the Offertory Prayer (*Receive, O Lord, this all-embracing host and wine, symbols of your creation, offered to you that they may be transformed into your New Creation*) or people depart after a prayer.

Sacred Heart of our own heart,
help us to realize ourselves as part of your cosmos.
May we reverence you in all things
and know ourselves as brothers and sisters of Christ,
the first-fruits of your new Creation.

This we ask in the name of that Heart
which is the womb of life and love.
Amen.

APPENDIX 1

Spiritual Direction

Spiritual direction is an ecumenical ministry whereby a person (often called a 'directee') is aided in their life in Christ by someone (a 'spiritual director') who is experienced in life's pilgrimage and has developed Godly wisdom. While some find 'direction/director' off-putting and prefer Accompaniment or Soul Friend all concern a ministry aiding our growth in Christ. People may use the sacrament of Confession (Appendix 5) but, while both require an individual to whom to open the heart, spiritual direction doesn't require a priest. Sin is the focus of Confession rather than the whole of a person's life in Christ and any 'advice' given is brief (if anything longer is appropriate the penitent might be advised to speak with their director) and dependent on being requested. They have a symbiotic relationship (connection), but spiritual direction cannot offer absolution. While both are confidential ministries that of the confessional is absolute, whereas a director is recommended to have (confidential) supervision for their ministry.

Spiritual direction emerged during the early monastic era when individuals sought out a Desert Elder to aid them. Today a director might be a Religious or clergyperson, but is often a layman or woman who has certain graces and abilities through their life in Christ, often aided by training in this ministry. They offer a welcoming, confidential, non-judgemental relationship in which to identify and explore what God is doing in the directee's life; a safe space in which to be honest, find woundedness accepted and where painful memories can be released. Recognizing the importance of the whole person (mind, body and spirit) and their life-context it differs from counselling, workplace supervision or mentoring in being the process of accompanying the directee on their journey and how they are being called into a deeper relationship with God.

What happens?

> *A typical session lasts up to an hour. The directee should consider how they want to use the time. One question to reflect on is 'What movements in my inner life have I noticed occurring since we last met? How have I been conscious – or not – of God's activity in my life?' The session would then continue with the director inviting you to consider open, reflective questions, working with you to deepen your experience of the movement of God, helping you come to that place of freedom whereby you can make your response to the One who is calling you to ever deeper union. At times there may be some insights offered as the director will also be noticing the way the Spirit is working in them. For, in the end, it is God who is the primary Director and both director and directee need to realize that they sit in that Divine, compassionate gaze. (John-Francis Friendship,* The Mystery of Faith, *p. 172)*

Most regions have someone responsible for helping people find a director. Further information is available via most diocesan websites or from https://www.lcsd.org.uk/, the Retreat Association (https://www.retreats.org.uk/spiritualdirection) or Spiritual Directors International (https://www.sdicompanions.org/).

APPENDIX 2

Heart Speaks to Heart (SH.2)
A Short Liturgy

This could be added to an Office or stand alone. An icon/ picture of the Sacred Heart should be the focal point.

After an initial greeting and suitable hymn:

Reading: Proverbs 4.10–23

Silence, followed by Psalm 73 or 139 *said slowly and antiphonally*

Reading: John 4.7–15

V   Blessed are the pure in heart;
R   for they shall see God.

Silence

Reading: John 19.31–37

V   The soldier thrust his lance into Jesus' side;
R   and immediately blood and water flowed out.
V   When he saw the crowds, Jesus had compassion for
    them, because they were harassed and helpless;
R   like sheep without a shepherd.
V   For to this end your side was pierced, your heart
    wounded;

R   so that through the visible wound we might see the invisible wound of your love. (*St Bonaventure*)

Confession

An appropriate act of sorrow and repentance followed by:

A reading for two voices from the Song of Songs 2.8f.:

1   The voice of my beloved! Look, he comes,
leaping upon the mountains, bounding over the hills.

2   **My beloved is like a gazelle or a young stag.**
Look, there he stands behind our wall,
gazing in at the windows, looking through the lattice.

1   My beloved speaks and says to me:
'Arise, my love, my fair one, and come away;
for now the winter is past, the rain is over and gone.

2   **The flowers appear on the earth;**
the time of singing has come,
and the voice of the turtle-dove is heard in our land.
Arise, my love, my fair one, and come away.

A Poem by Fr Andrew SDC:

To rest a tired head upon Thy Heart,
And to be still –
To come to Thee from the whole world apart
And learn Thy Will –
And in that will, because it is Thy will, to live and die,
Knowing Thy love and will are one eternally.
that be my way of prayer –
That brings me where Thou art –
Heaven is there.

Silence

Hymn

V1   O my dove, in the clefts of the rock,
       in the covert of the cliff,
       let me see your face, let me hear your voice;
All   **for your voice is sweet, and your face is lovely.**

Reading: Revelation 3.15–16

Reflection
Perfect devotion to the Heart of Jesus concerns detachment
from self and a continuous exercise of love for Jesus Christ:
'give me your grace and your love – this is enough for me'.

*The Blessed Sacrament is placed before people and a time
of silence follows after which the Sacrament is replaced,
followed by:*

Conclusion
Let us pray with one heart and mind: *Our Father ...*

Collect of the Sacred Heart

Blessing
Keep your heart with all vigilance,
for from it flow the springs of life. **Amen.**
Peace I leave with you; my peace I give to you.
I do not give to you as the world gives. **Amen.**
Do not let your hearts be troubled,
and do not let them be afraid. **Amen.**
And (may) the blessing of God, Father, ✠ Son and Holy Spirit
be with you now and always. **Amen.**

Go, in the peace of Christ. **Amen.**

APPENDIX 3

Consecration of a Group/Parish to the Sacred Heart of Jesus

The act of consecrating people, churches or parishes to the Sacred Heart is ancient and venerable. Just as every month has a specific dedication to help enrich our faith and focus our devotion so June is linked to the Sacred Heart. It aids the desire of a group (congregation) to develop their devotional life by renewing their dedication to the Love of God and commit themselves to nurturing a heart like his. The following could be used before the Blessing at the main Eucharist on the first Sunday in June.

A Litany of the Sacred Heart may be said before the statue of the Sacred Heart after which:

Let us pray:
Most sweet Jesus, Redeemer of the world,
look on us as we stand before you.
We are yours and we wish to remain so
and now consecrate ourselves to your Sacred Heart ...
   (brief silence)
Have mercy on all people,
especially those in need of knowing your compassionate and
   merciful love.
Be the inspiration and strength of the faithful
and of those who have given up hope.
May they know they are welcome in their Father's house.

Reconcile those who live in discord;
soften the hearts of those who have become hardened;
give hope to all who are lost;
bring joy to any living in torment of mind.
Bring those who worship here,
together with the whole world,
to cry with one voice:
Praise to the Divine Compassion
which brought about our salvation.
To your Sacred Heart we consecrate ourselves
[and this Parish/*Institution*]
to you be honour and glory for ever. **Amen.**

A PERSONAL ACT OF DEDICATION
TO DIVINE COMPASSION

Sacred Heart of Jesus, I consecrate myself to you;
Compassionate Heart of Jesus,
I place my sufferings with yours;
Strong Heart of Jesus, I entrust my weak heart to you;
Merciful Heart of Jesus,
I renounce all that might displease you;
Loving Heart of Jesus,
I look to you as my hope of salvation;
Wise Heart of Jesus,
I open my heart that it may learn from you;
Delightful Heart of Jesus,
I drink the waters of life from you;
Faithful Heart of Jesus,
grant me to remain enfolded in you now,
and at the hour of my death. Amen.
(Based on a prayer by St Margaret-Mary Alacoque)

APPENDIX 4

A Litany of the Sacred Heart of Jesus

(Amended form of the traditional Litany)

Lord, have mercy.
Christ, have mercy.
Lord, have mercy.

Christ, hear us.
Christ, graciously hear us.

God, the Father of Heaven, **have mercy on us.**
God, the Son, Redeemer of the world, **have mercy on us.**
God, the Holy Spirit, **have mercy on us.**
Holy Trinity, one God, **have mercy on us.**

Heart of Jesus, Son of the Eternal Father, **have mercy on us.**
Heart of Jesus, Word made flesh, **have mercy on us.**
Heart of Jesus, formed in the womb of Mary by the
   Holy Spirit, **have mercy on us.**
Heart of Jesus, filled with the Holy Spirit, **have mercy on us.**
Heart of Jesus, furnace of love, **have mercy on us.**
Heart of Jesus, fountain of life and holiness, **have mercy on us.**
Heart of Jesus, obedient until death, **have mercy on us.**
Heart of Jesus, drawing all peoples to yourself,
   have mercy on us.
Heart of Jesus, Temple of perpetual prayer, **have mercy on us.**
Heart of Jesus, penetrating and enlivening creation,
   have mercy on us.
Heart of Jesus, delight of the saints, **have mercy on us.**

Heart of Jesus, which is our treasure, **have mercy on us.**
Heart of Jesus, touched by our sins, **have mercy on us.**
Heart of Jesus, source of compassion, **have mercy on us.**
Heart of Jesus, source of consolation, **have mercy on us.**
Heart of Jesus, source of peace, **have mercy on us.**
Heart of Jesus, source of reconciliation, **have mercy on us.**
Heart of Jesus, reaching out to those in need,
   have mercy on us.
Heart of Jesus, hidden fountain of healing love,
   have mercy on us.
Heart of Jesus, longing for our unity, **have mercy on us.**
Heart of Jesus, enfolded in the Blessed Sacrament,
   have mercy on us.
Heart of Jesus, troubled by your Passion, **have mercy on us.**
Heart of Jesus, weeping over Jerusalem, **have mercy on us.**
Heart of Jesus, dying for love of us, **have mercy on us.**
Heart of Jesus, reaching into the darkness, **have mercy on us.**
Heart of Jesus, loving into life, **have mercy on us.**
Heart of Jesus, doorway to heaven, **have mercy on us.**
Heart of Jesus, source of all the virtues, **have mercy on us.**
Heart of Jesus, eternally present, **have mercy on us.**

Lamb of God, you take away the sins of the world,
   spare us, O Lord.
Lamb of God, you take away the sins of the world,
   graciously hear us, O Lord.
Lamb of God, you take away the sins of the world,
   have mercy on us, O Lord.

V   Jesus, meek and humble of Heart.
R   Make our hearts like yours.

Let us pray:
Almighty and everlasting God,
look upon the Heart of your beloved Son
and upon his life of loving mercy, prayer and praise
and, of your goodness, pardon those who seek your mercy,
in the name of your Son, Jesus Christ. **Amen.**

APPENDIX 5

THE SACRAMENT OF RECONCILIATION (or CONFESSION)

Many of us carry in our hearts the burden of unresolved anger, selfishness, ingratitude, pride, etc., and research into human psychology has shown how important it is to be able to deal with these matters, for unrepented sin binds us in its chains. We come to this sacrament bearing our load of guilt and shame and, admitting our faults with faith and trust that they will be taken away, hear Christ say through the voice of the priest to whom God has given the power of heavenly absolution, 'I forgive you your sins ...' While Confession isn't the same as therapy there are connections and many would be helped if they realized they could unload their burdens within the confidentiality of this sacrament.

All priests, through their ordination, are authorized to hear confessions and, although some think it is 'Roman Catholic', any baptized person may use this sacrament, *The Visitation of the Sick* (Book of Common Prayer) containing the following note: '... *the sick person shall be moved to make a special Confession of his sins, if he feel his conscience troubled with any weighty matter. After which the Priest shall absolve him (if he humbly and heartily desire it)* ...'.

The 'seal' of the confessional

Unlike other similar forms of ministry 'what's said in the confessional stays in the confessional': the priest is forbidden by the church's laws (which are upheld by Parliament) to reveal anything that's been confessed unless '... his *(sic)* own life may be called into question for concealing the same'. This requirement of absolute confidentiality applies even after the death of the penitent (the 'seal of the confessional') – a burden the confessor must carry.

While it is said that the Anglican attitude to Confession is 'All may, none must, some should', that shouldn't be understood as 'why bother' and those seeking to develop a closer relationship with God will discover the importance of this sacrament on the path to at-oneness with Jesus.

Preparing yourself

If it's your first Confession it would help to explain this to the priest beforehand (if not your own, then ask whom you might approach – and confessors themselves need to be regular penitents). In preparing for a first Confession set aside time for reflecting on your life ('examine your conscience'), which might be done over a few days or during your annual Retreat.

Begin by reading, for example, the Parable of the Two Sons (Luke 15.11–32) or the Beatitudes (Matthew 5.1f.) or Commandments (Exodus 20), asking the Holy Spirit to help you recognize how (often) you have sinned 'in thought, word and deed'. Consider the two brothers of the parable and how your life might be similar to theirs – make brief notes of what you recall ('I was angry with ... nursed jealousy on six/some/many occasions'; 'Once I cheated during an exam'; 'I twice lied about ...' ; 'I frequently look at pornography'; 'I once/twice ... stole ... from someone'). You need, briefly, to name what you repent of, desire not to repeat and for which you seek absolution. Be quite straightforward – nothing will shock a priest (who is also a sinner): remember, however, that you're ultimately speaking to Jesus who already knows your heart and forget the presence of the priest who, providing penitence and amendment of life are expressed, is there to declare absolution and offer advice (if requested).

What happens?

There are different ways in which confessions are heard and many places where they occur. Sometimes formal, sometimes not, whatever necessity dictates. Making your confession – being open and honest – may be a blessing in disguise, but it's a costly blessing … sin has a price. Many find it helpful to kneel before an image of the Crucified, sign of Christ's compassionate love, while the confessor is veiled from sight. You come with an awareness of dirt clinging to you and, often through the mist of tears, leave with a sense of having been cleansed.

After you've asked a blessing feel free to cross yourself as the priest responds (don't worry if you don't). There'll probably be a card available with words you can use such as, '*I confess to almighty God* …', which may be followed by, '*I accuse myself of the following sins*' – which is the hint to admit them. You'll end with a phrase such as: '*For these and all the other sins that I cannot remember I am heartily sorry, firmly mean to do better, most humbly ask pardon of God and of you, Father/Mother, penance (advice) and absolution. Amen.*' Contrition (sorrow) for what's been done, asking God's forgiveness and a real desire to amend one's life must be part of the process, for Confession isn't just about finding forgiveness, it's about desiring to change one's life and grow into greater Christ-likeness. The priest will then offer some encouraging words and suggest a simple penance, such praying a psalm, before offering absolution – the following is based on one in the 1662 Book of Common Prayer:

Our Lord Jesus Christ, who has left power to his Church
to absolve all sinners who truly repent and believe in him,
of his great mercy forgive you your offences:
And by his authority committed to me,
I absolve you from all your sins,
In the Name of the Father, ✠ and of the Son,
and of the Holy Spirit. Amen.

If possible you should make your act of penance as soon as
you leave the confessional. As you do so, give thanks that
Christ has taken away the burden of your sin – and joyfully
tear up your 'sin-list'!

Priests have received a power which God has given
neither to angels nor to archangels. It was said to them:
'Whatsoever you shall bind on earth shall be bound in
heaven; and whatsoever you shall loose, shall be loosed.'
... What greater power is there than this? The Father
has given all judgement to the Son. And now I see the
Son placing all this power in the hands of men. They are
raised to this dignity as if they were already gathered up
to heaven. (John Chrysostom, *The Priesthood*, 3:5)

Confession is an act of honesty and courage – an act of
entrusting ourselves, beyond sin, to the mercy of a loving
and forgiving God. (Pope St John Paul II)

Bibliography

al-Tirmidhi, Al-Hakim, 1947, *K. al-riyada-we-adab al-nafs*, A. J. Arberry.

Andrew SDC, Father, 1950, 'Echo of S Augustine', in *Prayers from Father Andrew*, ed. Kathleen E. Burne, Mowbray.

Barrett Browning, Elizabeth, 1864, *Aurora Leigh*, J. Miller.

Benson SSJE, Richard Meux, 1966, *Look to the Glory*, Society of St John the Evangelist, Canada.

Bryant SSJE, Christopher, 1980, *The Heart in Pilgrimage*, Darton, Longman & Todd.

Campbell, Roy, 1979, *Poems of St John of the Cross*, Fount.

Cripps, Arthur Shearly, 1939, *Africa: Verses*, Oxford University Press.

Croiset SJ, John, 2007, *The Devotion to the Sacred Heart*, TAN Books

de Chardin, Pierre Teilhard, 1918, *Mon Universe*, Éditions du Seuil.

de Chardin, Pierre Teilhard, 1960, *Le Milieu Divin*, Harper and Row.

de Chardin, Pierre Teilhard, 1965, *The Making of a Mind*, Harper Row.

de Chardin, Pierre Teilhard, 1980, *The Heart of Matter*, Harcourt Brace.

de Osuna, Francisco, 1981, *The Third Spiritual Alphabet*, tr. Mary E. Giles, Paulist Press.

de Saint-Exupéry, Antoine, 2019, *The Little Prince*, Egmont.

de Sales, Francis, 2009, *Introduction to the Devout Life*, Dover Pubs.

de Sales, Francis, 2011, *Treatise on the Love of God*, Wilder Pubs.

Dailey OSFS, Thomas, 2020, *Behold the Heart*, Sophia Inst. Press.

Delio, Ilya, 2013, *Simply Bonaventure*, New City Press.

Elizabeth, Mother, 1967, *Into the Deep*, The Confraternity of the Divine Love.

Friendship, John-Francis, 2019, *The Mystery of Faith*, Canterbury Press.

Kane, Thomas, 2022, *Gentleness in John of the Cross*, SLG Press.

Keen, Sam, 1991, *Fire in the Belly*, Bantam Books.

Kubicki SJ, James, 2012, *A Heart on Fire*, Ave Maria Press.

Linn, Sheila Fabricant (Matthew and Dennis Linn), 1994, *Healing Spiritual Abuse and Religious Addiction*, Paulist Press.

MacFarlane, Robert, 2020, *Underland: A Deep Time Journey*, Penguin Books.

Manton, Jo, 1977, *Sister Dora*, Quartet Books.

McLean, Julienne, 2023, *The Diamond Heart: Jungian Psychology and the Christian Mystical Tradtition*, Chiron Publications.

Metropolitan Anthony of Sourozh, 1986, *The Essence of Prayer*, Darton, Longman & Todd.

Nicholson, D. H. S. and Lee, A. H. E., eds, 1917, *The Oxford Book of Mystical Verse*, Clarendon Press.

Richo, David, 2007, *The Sacred Heart of the World*, Paulist Press.

Shaw, Gilbert, 1992, *A Pilgrim's Book of Prayers*, SLG Press.

Shepherd, Nan, 2011, *The Living Mountain*, Canongate Books.

Stewart OSB, Columba, 1986, *World of the Desert Fathers*, SLG Press.

Sviri, Sara, 1997, *The Taste of Hidden Things*, The Golden Sufi Center.

Teresa of Avila, 1995, *The Interior Castle*, Fount Paperbacks.

Theophan the Recluse, St, 2001, *Turning the Heart to God*, Conciliar Press.

Underhill, Evelyn, 2004, *Concerning the Inner Life with The House of the Soul*, Wipf and Stock.

Underhill, Evelyn, 1995, *Mysticism*, Bracken Books.

Underhill, Evelyn, 2013, *The Spiritual Life,* Martino Publishing.

Vaughan-Lee, Llewellyn, 2012, *Prayer of the Heart in Christian and Sufi Mysticism*, The Golden Sufi Center Publishing.

von Hildebrand, Dietrich, 2007, *The Heart: An Analysis of Human and Divine Affectivity*, St Augustine's Press.

Ward SLG, Sr Benedicta, 1992, *Discernment: A Rare Bird*, The Way Supplement 64.

Ware, Kallistos, 1979, *The Orthodox Way*, St Vladimir's Orthodox Theological Seminary.

Ware, Kallistos, 2001, *The Inner Kingdom*, St Vladimir Press.

Williams, Rowan, 2024, *Passions of the Soul*, Bloomsbury Continuum.

Wright, Wendy M., 2004, *Heart Speaks to Heart*, Darton, Longman & Todd.

Writings from the Philokalia, 1992, ed. E. Kadloubovsky, trans. G. E. H. Palmer, Faber and Faber.

Zacharias, Archimandrite, 2014, *The Hidden Man of the Heart*, Stavropegic Monastery of St John the Baptist.

Zacharias, Archimandrite, 2017, *The Engraving of Christ in Man's Heart*, Stavropegic Monastery of St John the Baptist.

OTHER BOOKS BY JOHN-FRANCIS FRIENDSHIP

ENFOLDED IN CHRIST: The inner life of a priest

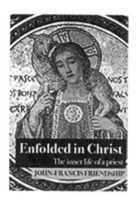

Inspired by words of St John Vianney, the Curé d'Ars, *'the priesthood is the love of the heart of Jesus'*, this book focuses on the 'being beneath the role' offering an aid for developing a healthy spiritual life for clergy, ordinands and those considering their call. It doesn't concern ministry, but draws on different spiritualities including Benedictine, Franciscan and Ignatian as it seeks to help ministers cultivate practices and habits that will nurture awareness of Christ, sustain holy living and foster personal wellbeing.

https://canterburypress.hymnsam.co.uk/
books/9781786220462/enfolded-in-christ

THE MYSTERY OF FAITH: *Exploring Christian belief*

Written for the average reader exploring the essentials of Christian Faith it is ideal for individuals or groups. Based on the 'Apostles' Creed it explores essentials and includes material on the nature of God, prayer, the sacraments, worship, Christian living, etc. It is divided into sections designed to facilitate discussion. Foreword by the Bishop of Salisbury.

Canterbury Press have produced a video: https://youtu.be/k114d_eVzPo

---

WHAT DO YOU SEEK? *Wisdom from Religious Life*

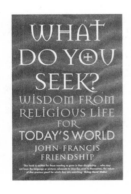

This focuses on our growth in Christ, what it means to be human and how we can live together. Although its primary concern isn't to promote the Life it does use stories concerning various (Anglican) Orders and would be of value to anyone wanting to deepen their faith or those considering their calling. Chapters concern the wisdom of the Desert Elders and monastic way; contemplative and kingdom living; prayer and how the Life informs both the ordained and those seeking to live life in Christ. Finally, it addresses 'the Hidden monk' (nun) in the depths of us all.

https://canterburypress.hymnsam.co.uk/
books/9781786223456/what-do-you-seek

DAILY PRAYER AND DIVINE OFFICE

An 80 page booklet published by Darton, Longman and Todd aimed at anyone:

- wanting to 'go deeper' as they pray the Office;
- in formation for ordained ministry or Religious Life;
- for whom the Office has become stale and who need to be refreshed in realizing the treasures it offers.

Not limited to any particular version it offers short chapters on the development of the Office, suggestions on how to pray the psalms, devotional approaches, suggestions as to how it can enrich ones prayer life, etc. *Reduced price copies are available from jff2209@yahoo.com*

CRUX YOUTUBE VIDEOS

concerning matters of Faith by John-Francis Friendship

https://youtube.com/playlist?list=
PL80GzQeQSHzlrHZeBmlNdVEtLscrSfYw3